Top Teamwork

Master Team Building and Management at Your Workplace by Using the Skills Learned in This Book

OSCAR STONE

TABLE OF CONTENTS

Top Teamwork

TABLE OF CONTENTS

The Most Critical Core Values of a Successful Team

(Never lead a team without these 7 values…)

<u>Why is it important to set Team Values?</u>

Values define what your company cares about. They represent the goals and intentions of an organisation, and tell employees how their work spirit should look like. If the wrong values are set, overall productivity and work relationships will get damaged.

To receive your Team Values List for **free**, visit this link:

<u>https://starkingbooks.activehosted.com/f/1</u>

Introduction

There's a lot going on within team dynamics. Nowadays, teams consist of a wide range of talent, from employees who work on-premise to employees who work remotely. Thanks to the technology sandstorm of the 20th century, members of the same organisation could even be working in a different country or continent. So how do you make sure that your team remains motivated at work and that the company runs like a well-oiled machine? How do you cultivate an atmosphere of positive energy at the workplace where employees can come in, every day feeling excited and inspired to give their best effort? By encouraging *great teamwork*.

You see, teamwork is the essence of all organisations, big or small. The group of people who unite to achieve a common goal will be the deciding factor as to whether a business succeeds or not. Members of the team must work together effectively with one aim in mind, and that is to increase performance and productivity, or the company isn't going to survive for very long.

But how does such a top team come about? Employees spend most of their time, several hours a day, five days a week, at work. A positive, comfortable work environment is crucial to overall motivation and therefore, success. At the workplace, all members should work together instead of against one another. A motivated team embraces challenges and enjoys problem-solving because they know they have the opportunity to combine different solutions, talents, and abilities into one big productive final solution. In an ideal team scenario, new ideas flourish, and goals are achieved much faster, thanks to the varied group of skillsets present.

Is creating such a team dynamic possible? *Absolutely,* especially when a smart leader is sitting at the head of the team. He/She is the person who's responsible for overseeing all of this. Every team needs someone who leads and guides the group. Whether you're in the position of a boss or you're simply a member of the team with a natural inclination to take charge of situations, leaders make sure that the unit holds together and becomes the highest calibre team possible.

People are capable of extraordinary accomplishments, but they rarely ever achieve this on their own. Behind every success story are the people who have had a hand in shaping that story, each with a role to play. Some of the greatest achievements in history have been the end result of the *greatness of many*. It was never about one person doing it all. It was about a team of people who came together beautifully, to create a legacy of success that lives on for years to come. That's the power of great leadership and teamwork.

Everything that you *need* to become a great *leader* and to harness the *power of teamwork* is within the next few chapters. Achieving a great team dynamic is not as difficult as it seems, despite the diversity and different personalities involved, and it all starts with the decision to stop managing and *start leading* effectively.

In leadership, a wealth of knowledge is waiting to be used. With the right tools and strategies on hand, everyone is able to make better teamwork happen. I certainly was lacking these strategies and tools at the beginning of my career. But after some years of trial and error, I started to understand team dynamics and how to lead successfully. Learning from my mistakes and experiences is what brought me to the point where I am now, and I'm grateful for all the ups and downs throughout my journey. There's a lot of value and wisdom to be gained from experience, and that's why I decided to write this book.

I have been working with Start-ups and Big Business alike for close to 2 decades now. In this time, I've noticed some management tactics—what works and what doesn't. More so than anything else, I learned that people just want to feel validated, they want to feel worth it. It's very similar to the relationship I have with my daughter or my wife. At the end of the day, we are all just human beings, and we want to relate to each other as such, as equals. I've noticed an increasing rise in this trend as the generational shift within the workforce occurs. And that's the reason why new leaders must evolve with the time.

After spending the past six years working for a top-notch marketing agency in the UK, where I managed five different generations of workers at once, I felt compelled to share my valuable insight. This book is my hope to help you bypass the mistakes I've made, and be able to step boldly into your role as a team leader.

CHAPTER 1:

Where Does Teamwork Start?

*E*veryone can make a difference; every person can encourage top teamwork. Teamwork is like a fruit tree; the beautiful treetop is based on a firmly rooted trunk. Without that trunk, the branches wouldn't be able to hold together, and the whole tree would fall apart. But if the trunk keeps its ground and makes sure that the leaves and flowers get enough water, it enables the tree to bear fruit as a unit. The same goes for teamwork. Only if a strong leader supports and fuels the whole team, will they achieve the desired results. Every person can become the trunk of a tree; great leadership is not about "position," it is about *who you are*. You need to be authentic and pure in every action and intention that you carry out. And that's exactly where great teamwork starts.

Even if you're not in a leadership position just yet, if you stay true to who you are, sooner or later along the way, you will find other like-minded individuals who align with the goals and the values that you have.

They will be more than willing to follow you if they see your potential. John C. Maxwell, American speaker and author, once said: *"A leader is someone who knows the way, goes the way and shows everyone else the way."* Leadership is something that cannot be forced. If you do, you will fail every time. The problem is, the real message of what it means to be a great leader has been lost over the years.

Google what it means to be a great leader, or simply the term "leadership," and what you'll get back is millions of results within a second. It's easy to get lost in all that information. The more "stuff" you're faced with, the harder it can be to find the thing that you're looking for. In this case, that would be useful information. Sifting through so many different websites, blogs, journals, articles, research, and more telling you what leadership is and what you should or *should not* be doing, is enough to make anyone's head spin. Thousands of leadership concepts and models now exist and contribute to this complex tapestry that instead of helping us, it may end up confusing us more than ever. You could try to follow all the suggestions you come across, but if you're not true to who you are, you are still going to fail at the end of the day.

What Is Leadership?

Sun Tzu, who wrote the *Art of War,* believed that a leader works best when people barely know he exists. When a great leader is present, the job fulfilled, and the goal accomplished; the people believe *"we did it ourselves."* Coming back to the tree example, actually, the branches are the ones who are bearing and holding the fruits, but it's the trunk that makes it possible in the first place.

Sun Tzu wrote this: *"The General who advances without coveting fame and retreats without fearing disgrace, whose only thought is to protect the country and do service for his sovereign, is the jewel of the Kingdom."* The *Art of War* is among the many must-read books of today's top leaders for a reason. The Roman consul, Cicero, in the first century understood that a leader can only deliver results if he does it through other people and that he had to focus his attention on others if he wanted anything to happen or change. All of these wise scholars and philosophers believed that leadership was not about dominion; leadership was about service.

On the other hand, in the 16th century, Niccolo Machiavelli decided to write the book called *The Prince* in which he stated that everything was "all about the leader." Machiavelli believed that the leader must maintain power at all costs, and the focus must be entirely upon them, that they had to retain control by force or deceit if need be. Machiavelli's approach is both confusing and contradictory to what great leadership should be, and unfortunately, we are still clearing up his misconception of leadership today. Another bad example is Scott Thomas Carlyle (British Historian), who believed that leaders were born and not made. You either had the makings of a great leader, or you did not. If you had it, then you had the power to achieve greatness. If you did not? Well, that was too bad for you. You were either a leader or a follower, according to Carlyle. These beliefs have lingered on today like a bad smell that won't go away, and they have muddied the waters of what effective leadership looks like.

Leadership is actually very simple. It's not easy, but it is simple. Leadership is more about *who you are than what you do*, and it comes down to a few elementary rules. If you're able to grasp these rules and put them into practice, it's going to be impossible *not to inspire* others. But effective leadership can be nerve-wracking. Being a great leader to a team of people who are counting on you to encourage them, to steer them in the right direction is an even more overwhelming task. It's a lot of responsibility, and a leader is one that can effectively manage their team and bring out the best in everyone that is under their guidance. A successful leader is one who knows how to spearhead the journey to success. They are the ones who consistently act with honesty and integrity.

No matter which leadership position you hold, whether it's in a company, a sports team, an army, or any scenario in which you're in charge of a group of people, without integrity and honesty, you will never achieve true success. You must demonstrate the ability to stand by your core values and beliefs, and only when your followers see that they can place their trust in you will they become confident in your leadership abilities. So what makes a great leader? As I've learned through the path of my career, several things, to be honest.

The best leaders don't create more followers, they create more great leaders.

Let's start with the number one principle of leadership: *It's not about you.* Every step you take as a leader moving forward starts from this one principle. Eleanor Roosevelt said: *"A good leader can inspire people to have confidence in the leader. A great leader can inspire people to have confidence in themselves."* A leader is only a leader when they have followers, so there is a temptation to try and create more of a following. To gather more people who need you for the answers you can provide. But the best leaders don't create more followers. They are the ones who create more great leaders. They realise that they are not the hero of the day who swoops in and solves all the problems and answers all the questions. The world is too complex for just one person to have all the answers, yet a lot of people still believe that is what leaders are supposed to do.

Leaders are the people who never stop developing, achieving, and growing. They have the willpower to prevent themselves from getting stuck and too cosy in their comfort zone (the great danger area of success), and they are lifelong students. They *never stop learning,* even if they happen to be the subject matter expert in their field. Out of all the leadership qualities you read about, the hardest journey is identifying what the qualities you'll have to cultivate and learn to become a successful leader. No matter which way you define it, though, one thing you can be sure of is that a good leader can mean the difference between victory and failure.

All great leaders have a healthy mix of several qualities that contribute to their overall success. To become a great leader, you must:

- Always long to improve
- Identify the traits you are lacking
- Believe in your abilities
- Focus on doing things of greater value
- Hold yourself accountable
- Be a great contributor
- Be able to handle pressure
- Demonstrate mutual respect
- Be a role model

Let's take a look at each of these characteristics, and I'll show you why they are essential in order to become a successful team leader.

Always Long to Improve

Never be satisfied. The key trait in building the leadership qualities that will propel you to success is to continually learn by taking courses, reading books, watching TED Talks and listening to podcasts. Always read and always study. No matter how busy they are, the best leaders are the ones who are readers. The *average CEO reads 52 books*, and they do that within a year. That's one book every week! Most people struggle to finish one book a month, let alone a week. Leaders never stop learning, and they never compromise on reading.

Identify the Traits You Are Lacking

Leaders are not afraid to admit they have weaknesses. What qualities are you missing right now as a leader? Only when you know what's missing can you then work on making it better. People are not born with all the qualities they need to be a leader. No, they work on building it as they go along. They deliberately work on cultivating the skills that they need. As the 6th President of the United States, John Quincy Adams once said, *"You're a leader if your actions inspire others to learn more, dream more, become more and do more."* Work hard at building and strengthening the qualities you're missing, work on what you think you need. If a quality is missing, work on it until you've mastered it—master one quality before you move onto the next.

Believe in Your Abilities

Don't worry about what happened in the past or the mistakes that were made. The future is what matters. If you have never been a leader before, it doesn't mean that you can't become one in the future. Before you can lead others, you need to be confident enough in your own ability to do so. Other people are not going to follow your leadership and commands if you are not sure about the decisions you make yourself. No one is going to believe in a leader who's regularly nervous and second-guessing their own decisions.

An effective leader needs always to display both *confidence and assertiveness*, a strength that others can take comfort in. You don't have to be overconfident, but you do need to reflect a certain degree of confidence, which allows your followers to develop trust in you as a leader. Leaders know what they want and then set out to make it happen.

Focus on Doing Things of Greater Value

Focus on the things that are going to add value and deliver results. That's what great leaders do. Read more, listen more, exercise more patience, whatever it takes. While you're doing that, you'll need to deliberately spend less time on activities that are going to impede your success, or that don't help you move ahead faster. *Focus on doing what you do for the future.* It's time to take a step back and look at your current priorities and strategies, what's working and what is only a distraction. If something isn't working and hasn't been for a while, it's time to rethink it and stop wasting any more time on it.

Hold Yourself Accountable

Being a leader is a lot of responsibility. As the one in charge, making decisions is going to be part of your leadership responsibilities. You must demonstrate the ability to make the right decisions when the time calls for it, and this is no easy feat. Every choice you make has a consequence, an impact on you and the people under your leadership. You must think carefully about every decision you want to make because once the wheels are in motion, you're going to have to stand by your choice. If there's a lot at stake, it might be best to get the opinions of others who have a major stake in the decision too.

Former businessman Arnold H. Glasgow said: *"A good leader is someone who takes a little more than their fair share of the blame, and a little less than their share of the credit."* That's what it means to be a leader. You're accountable for what you and your followers do. When they struggle, you struggle along with them, and when they succeed, give them the credit and acknowledgement they deserve for a job well done. If they stumble, work with them to see how you can improve. John Maxwell states that there are five levels of leadership; he says people follow because:

- ♦ **They Have To -** If you're the boss, they have no choice but to do as they're told.
- ♦ **They Like You -** They follow you because of how they feel about you.
- ♦ **You Deliver -** Your accomplishments speak for themselves, and it has inspired confidence in them.

- ◆ **You Help Them Grow -** They follow you because of what you have done for them and the way you've inspired them to be their best.
- ◆ **Of Who You Are -** They follow you because of who you are, and what you stand for and represent.

Each of these five layers forms a deeper level of commitment. In today's ever-changing world, it's not enough to be just one or the other anymore.

Be a Great Contributor

People are going to be looking at you to guide them, and they won't be motivated to do their best if their leader doesn't display the same passion and commitment towards achieving that goal. When a leader is not afraid to roll up his sleeves and *get his hands dirty too*, others will follow suit because of the dedication and the desire for getting the job done that is being demonstrated. To earn the respect of your followers, this is how you do it. Without commitment and passion, it's going to be an uphill task for any leader to keep the motivational fire going.

Be Able to Handle Pressure

A leader who runs around like a chicken with its head cut off whenever a crisis or problem crops up is no leader at all. An effective leader is someone who can *keep a clear head*. You're going to face some problems along the way, that's inevitable, and if you handle it well, your people will begin to trust that you can do this.

Demonstrate Mutual Respect

An effective leader constantly encourages and helps their followers overcome challenges faced without belittling them. A leader must respect their followers to gain honour in return. *Respect needs to be earned*, never demanded. When leaders don't appreciate their followers and vice versa, things can unravel really quickly, and not in a positive way. The best type of leaders and managers are ones that provide a work environment where employees help each other and value the contributions that everyone makes.

Be a Role Model

You need to be the change you desire to see in the world. If you want to create positive change, it all starts with you and the way you lead others to follow in your footsteps. As a leader, everyone is looking to you for guidance, and it is you that they take their orders from.

Practice what you preach because your people are watching what you do. If you insist on your team being punctual, then you need to ensure that you are punctual too. If you remain calm and cool in stressful situations, your team will do the same. You need to be someone that your team can look up to, admire and respect.

Leaders vs. Managers

Disney's *Ratatouille* movie brought to light an interesting concept; that a leader can come from anywhere, even a rat with a dream and a passion.

There's no such thing as 100% management or 100% leadership because an organisation needs both of them. Leaders have a more effective approach to communication rather than controlling. A leader needs to have excellent communication skills, or it's going to be very hard to explain your vision and tell the team what needs to be done to accomplish a goal. Words are powerful enough to inspire, motivate, and make people push past their boundaries, accomplishing things they never thought possible. When leaders use the power of good communication skills, there's no telling what they can inspire their team to achieve (we'll talk more about communication in another chapter).

Leaders create followers, and managers manage people and things.

Leaders are focused on taking the organisation from Point A to B. They also are known for taking risks, instead of maintaining the status quo and keeping things steady. Leaders are trying to stretch the organisation past what it's currently doing, and thereby growing it bigger and stronger. Leaders are also much more people-focused and relationship-focused. They do more mentoring, coaching or teaching. Leaders have the ability to communicate persuasively, inspiring vision, and getting people excited about the future.

Managers, on the other hand, have more of a control mindset. They're focused on the administration of processes and the structure and the resources of the organisation. They're very task-focused and much into maintaining the status quo, so maintenance is a key part of what they do. Overall, managers are working on the day to day tasks and making sure that everything gets done in an orderly fashion. While managers certainly have a lot of important communication functions, they're more inclined to go with the by-the-book approach.

Leaders create followers, and managers manage people and things. That is the easiest way to remember it. Some great leaders of today exhibit all the qualities needed, and that is why they will always be remembered for their visionary approach.

Nelson Mandela

The former leader of the Anti-Apartheid movement, Mandela, exhibited tremendous resilience, focus, determination and willpower, even though his actions landed him in prison. He was willing to stand by what he believed in, and he became the reason South Africa has a free and equal future. He stayed true to who he was, even when he was met with consequences that would have made any other men quit.

Jeff Bezos

Jeff Bezos built his empire on a foundation of innovation and experimentation, and his leadership style is mostly known for the customer-first approach and his long-term vision. In 1999 Bezos explained that he wants Amazon to become Earth's most customer-centric company where customers can find everything they may want to buy online. And this vision still holds true today. For example, during some meetings, he orders one chair empty to represent the Amazon customer which should constantly remind the attendees that the customer is the most important person in the room. Bezos enthusiastic persona (which was compared to a start-up boss trying to make his first payroll) inspires his employees to believe in the vision of Amazon and make it a reality.

Dalai Lama

He is known for relentlessly and tirelessly campaigning for peace, reconciliation, democracy, and nonviolence. Even after 50-years of doing this, the Dalai Lama still persists with passion for his cause. The Dalai Lama simply radiates with charm and charisma and left little doubt over his influence when he won the Nobel Peace Prize in 1989. Based on his Twitter account, he has 19.3 million followers looking to him for guidance. That speaks for itself.

Jack Ma

Ma was never afraid to think outside the box. That's why he decided to start an online business, despite being unable to access the internet in his hometown. After repeatedly changing business models, he founded the e-commerce store Alibaba. Shortly after the foundation, Ma told a journalist: *"We don't want to be number one in China. We want to be number one in the world."* Ever since Alibaba was founded, Ma continues to be a strong advocate of the "think big" approach, which he encourages all his employees to partake in. Leaders are all about change and the willingness to break the rules. For example, did Ma persuade organisations to invest millions of dollars in his company without even being able to present a business plan. He pioneered his company to become one of the world's largest businesses online and a renowned name worldwide.

Zhang Ruimin

It was Ruimin's willingness to be radical with his innovations that turned Haier from a company that was once small and failing to among the world's biggest names in household appliances. Ruimin's approach to leadership is to group his employees into smaller teams that manage themselves and even elect their own leaders, a concept that is still unheard of in China and still considered an unusual approach in the Western world. And this is exactly what makes Ruimin a great leader because he is willing to take risks and make moves that others are hesitant to do.

Howard Schultz

The CEO of Starbucks is considered ahead of most CEO's because he understood that he wasn't selling a product. Schultz knew that he was selling an *experience* to the customer. His concept involved inviting décor, calming music and speedy Wi-Fi so everyone would feel at home. He was able to imagine Starbucks as a place that was the most-visited after home and work, whereas other food/drink stops look more like grab-and-go. Schultz saw the value in focusing beyond only the sales numbers and creating a pleasant environment for the customer.

As different as leaders and managers are, both these roles have their importance and purpose. Sometimes you have to be a good manager as well as a leader, especially if you're in any kind of small business or team setting.

Visionary leaders will hire good task-oriented managers to balance out the team. This goes back to principle number one, where it's *not all about you*. There's only so much you can do as a leader, and you need to understand what your team requires to function better. If your organisation *needs a manager* to help you oversee the team while you handle other affairs, then you need to hire one. A leader is not afraid to admit when they need help, and they're willing to listen and consider the needs of their team.

Unlike a manager who leads with completion, a leader chooses to lead with empathy and connection. You could decide to go with the dictatorial approach to leadership, and that may get things done, but that won't make you a great leader. A leader can never make truly meaningful connections if empathy is not present. Being an effective leader means you need to be able to put yourself in your team's shoes and understand their concerns. With that understanding, you're one step closer to making a difference in their lives and performance. That's how you become one of the greats that people will be willing to look up to and follow.

CHAPTER 2:

What You Definitely Should Not Be Doing

*L*eadership is like a double-edged sword. Do it well, and you could achieve unimaginable greatness, leaving behind a legacy that lasts a lifetime. Do it wrong, and you'll be remembered for all the wrong reasons. What's worse, poor leadership on your part could lead you to lose some of the best talents in your organisation. There will be certain individuals who stand out, and they usually establish themselves as team leaders in the workplace. They have vision, charisma, goals, and problem-solving capabilities and strategies. But that alone is not enough.

Focus on leading with the positive characteristics we talked about while being aware of the following destructive activities so that you can avoid these mistakes.

The Cost of Poor Leadership

There is no such thing as a bad team—only a bad leader. If right now, your team is not stepping up, it could be because you are not leading them to step up. If you have a toxic person in your team that sabotages the whole organisation, you need to fire that person. It's the leader's job to put together the best team possible in the first place.

Weak leaders blame everybody else, and they adopt the "victim mentality" approach. Once again, it's no all about you. Bad leaders inflict an air of superiority over their people, and they will never succeed in their role because no one will ever respect a leader who makes it difficult to be likeable. Remember, like the trunk, you want to be supportive, not superior. When you choose not to be humble, you soften your self-awareness, because you will be blinded to your own faults. Bad leaders often have an inflated ego, and the only thing they care about is their personal gain. They want approval for themselves. They're focused on how they can benefit rather than thinking about the people they are leading.

Leadership sets the tone for *everything* in an organisation. The culture, the standards, the performance, the outcomes, it all leads back to leadership. An environment with poor leadership becomes soulless. People forget why they started working for the company in the first place. You'll know that you're probably guilty of being a lousy leader if your team disperses as soon as you arrive. No leader is perfect, but some of the following leadership mistakes could be avoided entirely if the leaders are aware of what they may be doing wrong. These mistakes are:

- You have no vision
- A lack of integrity
- Overthinking
- Thinking you have all the answers
- Trying to micromanage your people
- Not broadening your perspective
- A lack of love
- Your team is not comfortable around you

You Have No Vision

While several mistakes contribute to poor leadership style, the *number one* factor why you fail as a leader is because you lack a compelling vision. A vision helps you define the kind of reputation you want your business to be associated with and where you see yourself in the future. What kind of impression do you want to leave? What do you want to be remembered for? You have to set the idea, to connect everyone to that mission, to inspire people to collaborate and elevate themselves to a new standard of performance.

A lack of vision equals failure every single time. Your people want to see progress. They want to know that their efforts and hard work are paying off, and they are moving forward. They want something to aspire towards, but a leader without a vision is someone who cannot provide these things for their people.

A Lack of Integrity

Once your followers figure out who you are (and it won't take them long to do it) and realise you lack integrity and transparency, you're not going to remain in the leadership position for very long. No one likes a shady leader and someone that they feel they cannot put their trust. Trust and respect go a long way in successful and effective leadership, and if your team doesn't respect you or trust you as a leader, your team will be doomed right from the start with no hope of success.

Overthinking

A simple matter which could be resolved easily could potentially get blown out of proportion if a leader reacts to it in a highly emotional way. One of the reasons people generally become more sensitive than they should is because they tend to overthink a lot of things. Avoid overthinking situations and just *see things for what they are.* You do that by looking at the facts in front of you. If something is not an objective fact, then don't think about it. Observe the situation in front of you, don't embellish, don't assume, don't add on "facts" of your own. This is how things get more complicated than they should, and emotions get fired up when there was no need to be.

Thinking You Have All the Answers

It's just as bad as overthinking. A leader who thinks they have all the answers is a leader who is missing out on a great learning opportunity. Even if you believe that you do have all the answers and maybe you do, you should still listen to what your team or anyone who approaches you with a suggestion or solution has to say. Great leaders are the ones who are *willing to listen*. Bad leaders are the ones who brush others off and insist on things being done their way. Do that and you'll never discover if there was indeed a better way you could have taken, an approach that would have opened the door to new possibilities and opportunities.

Trying to Micromanage Your People

Micromanaging happens when a leader does not trust the capabilities of the team. They treat their team like children that need to be watched and monitored throughout the day. A sign of poor leadership is when you tell your employees exactly how they should do certain tasks. You don't trust that they can do the work in their own way, and you think that your team must use your techniques because they're better than everyone else's. Maybe their method works better than you thought it would.

Not Broadening Your Perspective

In a world that is increasingly more globalised today than it has ever been, leadership's evolution arises onto a new plateau. To enter the team floor, a leader needs to *be open-minded* now more than ever. One of the biggest mistakes you could make as a leader would be to confine your circle to only people who talk, act, speak, and look like you do. An effective leader with a broader view of the world develops the ability to see things from multiple points of view, which then helps them make better, informed decisions to ensure the best possible outcome.

A Lack of Love

Leadership, by definition, isn't about trying to do something great as a lone ranger. It's about inspiring others to share the dream, and then creating the circumstances so that they can do the absolute best work. This is impossible to achieve if the leaders themselves lack passion and heart. Today, we are not in Business-to-Customer or Business-to-Business businesses. We are in the *People-to-People* business.

We are there to serve people. You have to communicate with love, and this is the best-kept secret of successful leaders. *Love*. To love what you do, remain in love with your leadership role, staying in love with your people, staying in love with your customers, staying in love with your organisation, and coming from the right place. Understanding your team members on a deep heartfelt level, always do the right thing because you know that's what you should be doing, treating your employees like family members. That's authentic leadership.

Your Team Is Not Comfortable Around You

Employees will leave if they have a weak leader at the helm of the ship, no matter how much they love their jobs. Your followers need to feel comfortable enough to be able to voice their opinions and concerns. If they are having difficulty working with another member of their team, they need to feel comfortable enough to approach you and bring up those concerns without worrying that there are going to be repercussions for themselves. As a leader, you need to establish yourself as a trustworthy figure and *encourage an open-door policy* among the people you are managing, helping them and making them feel safe whenever they approach you with a problem.

Before we continue, I wanted to mention that it is crucial to understand all of these mistakes so that you don't fall for them. Be smart and learn from the failures of others; this way, you can save yourself a lot of time and energy. Make better use of these valuable resources, and avoid the problems above. In this regard, here a few more you should be aware of:

- A lack of resources
- Overworking your team
- Valuing profits more than people
- Not connecting with your people
- Failing to delegate
- Being slow to act and adapt
- Forgetting to focus on the customer

A Lack of Resources

Are you providing your team with everything that they need? *Do you equip them for success?* When a leader fails to provide adequate resources for that team to be successful, the group as a whole is going to fail. It is the job of the leader to provide funding, technology, resources, influence staffing, whatever else is needed for those projects and those operational responsibilities to be considered successful.

Overworking Your Team

Overworking the best employees on the team is how you burn them out. Unfortunately, this is something weak leaders are guilty of because they become too comfortable relying on the most dependable members of their team. While the hardworking, performing members of the team no doubt should be praised, when piling on too much work, your team will start drifting towards the negative energy zone, and find themselves feeling tired or burned out.

Valuing Profits More Than People

The minute a leader and an organisation start to value their bottom line more than the people who work hard for them, is when the best employees pack up and leave. Sir Richard Branson (Head of Virgin Group Ltd.) is one leader who is famous for his *"people first" approach* and ensuring his team is always happy in their jobs. When a leader does not recognise the value and contribution of their people, they fail to motivate them, and once an employee has had enough, they'll hand in their resignation.

Not Connecting with Your People

Your team is more than just resources who were hired to get the job done for you. They are people too. Another big mistake that gets made by poor leadership is failing to connect to the employee as a *person*. Treating your team as a means to an end is what bad managers do. They shouldn't even be called leaders if this is the approach that they resort to.

Failing to Delegate

A bad leader will try to do it all because they believe they can do it better and realise too late that they should have delegated their tasks after all. Failure to entrust and spread the work evenly among your team, playing to each member's strengths is one of the costs of poor leadership. It is often the team that ends up paying the price for this one. They fail to meet deadlines, and the job is not done as well as it could have been.

Part of being an effective leader is knowing the *strengths and weaknesses of your team members* and then behaving in a way that draws all of the positive qualities together. A good leader is one that delegates the right job to the right people, so they come away with excellent results because they know exactly what to do when a task is given to them. People have been known to become better performers and become more engaged staff when they feel they are really excelling at the tasks at hand, and you would be surprised at just how much this can impact the productivity of a team.

Being Slow to Act and Adapt

The fear of making mistakes could be one of the traits that turn a potentially good leader into a bad one. Decisions need to be made quickly and sometimes on the spot depending on the challenge you're faced with. And a leader who is too slow or too afraid to make a move quickly enough to stay one step ahead will always find themselves two steps behind everybody else.

Forgetting to Focus on The Customer

When the leader fails to pay attention to what the need of his customers is, they are destined for failure. It's not only the employees that they need to focus on, but it's the customers too—the people who help to keep the business alive, besides the employees. A customer is *the financial lifeline of the company*, and when your customers are gone, so are you. A leader who excels at what they do is one that thinks about the customer experience more so than the bottom line. They think about how to inspire loyalty and satisfaction among the customer, the same way they try to do for their team. Ignoring the needs of others is the quickest way to ensure that your days in that leadership position are numbered.

The Charm of Great Leadership

Now that you know the characteristics you should steer clear from, let's look at the qualities of a good leader. As a leader, you must develop the ability to be introspective. Introspection allows you to reflect on your actions thus far, and the contributions you've made. How you've influenced others, what your goals are, and what purposeful role you may play in your life at this point. Introspection forces you to confront what's happening within you internally, so you can no longer deny or ignore all the thoughts and emotions you may have tried to run away from for so long. In doing so, you become enlightened, and you can free yourself from the shackles of ignorance.

Take hold of this introspection and begin to look towards the qualities that will turn you into a leader, and people will be more than happy to follow.

Have Courage

You must be willing to take risks to reach your goals even if you're not guaranteed success. There is no certainty in life or business. Every commitment and action you make will always entail some kind of risk or consequence. In your leadership, there are going to be moments that push you beyond your limits. Moments that challenge you, and threaten to defeat you, testing your will to see what you're made of. It is for this reason that you must develop courage and inner strength to be able to weather the storm and still exhibit self-control and positivity despite the difficulties faced. Courage is going to be one of your most outwardly identifiable traits.

Treat Your People Like Unique Individuals

It's easy to think of your team as a whole unit, forgetting that each member of the group is a unique individual in their own right. They all have a different perspective, approach, and unique view, each one with something to offer if you know how to recognise their individual contributions and strengths. To be an effective leader that solves problems for good, so it doesn't keep recurring, you need to tailor your solutions depending on the person you are dealing with. Although two people may face a similar problem, the way that they approach or handle the problem will be very different because they are two diverse personalities. The issue will be perceived individually and, as such, affect them differently in the process. Treat them as individuals *first* and a team second.

Be Humble

Humility is going to be one of your greatest traits as a leader. Great leaders are decisive and strong, yet humble at the same time. Humility is not a weakness or a lack of self-confidence. It means that you have the courage and awareness needed to recognise the strength and value that others have, and you don't feel threatened about it. A great leader is someone who encourages and nurtures the talent that surrounds them, even if it means there could be some who end up being better than they are; they don't let their ego get in the way. Why? Because a good leader understands that it is not about them, it is about the overall organisation as a whole and everyone involved. This is why an effective leader is one that cultivates the team dynamic. Be humble because it's okay to admit you may have made a mistake. It's okay to admit you don't know all the answers.

Give Your Team a Purpose

Like already mentioned, great leaders *must have a vision*. This is a non-negotiable quality that cannot be compromised. They must be able to look ahead, be clear, and excited about the idea of where they're going and what they're trying to accomplish. Like a general in war, leaders must hone their strategic planning skills to turn this vision into reality. Leaders and successful individuals rise each morning with a sense of purpose, and they pass this purpose on to their team. This will keep your team's motivation going—this part of the strategic planning quality that all great leaders need.

Prioritise and Plan

Being able to prioritise enables you to have a clear sense of direction, and it always ensures that the most important things of all don't slip through the rungs without the need for micromanaging. Leaders make lists, and then they make a note of the tasks, which they need to prioritise. Successful leaders rarely ever do things on a whim. To stay on track, priorities need to be set, and work needs to get done according to those priorities. That's the only way to go about it.

Every thought, action, and the decision must be carefully mapped out and planned down to the last detail. This is how people remain more productive, how they stay so focused on what they need to do, and how they remain motivated to accomplish their goals. Leaders always exhibit a lot of organisation and planning in their day because they know they are responsible for other individuals; they know people are looking towards them to lead the way.

Don't Be Afraid to Ask Questions

As already mentioned, being a leader doesn't mean you need to have the answers to everything. Questions give you the answers that you need, and you should never feel awkward or embarrassed at having questions on your mind. Part of the greatness of a leader is the ability to take other people's advice and appreciate when someone was able to present a solution. This isn't something that all leaders can do. A leader who is willing to ask questions will *always* be a better leader than someone who pretends to know it all. The latter will usually end up being too bossy and domineering instead of empowering.

A dynamic, hardworking, successful team is one that runs like a well-oiled machine. Every cog to the wheel of your team enters smoothly into its gear to achieve a harmonious result. That can only happen under the helm of great leadership, and that kind of team dynamic is something you need to *create by design*. It doesn't happen by default. It occurs through the actions and decisions you decide to (or not to) do.

Listening to what your team needs is the easiest way to decide what to do. Not only will you know what to improve on, but also will your team feel more acknowledged. If you were an employee, would you want a leader who is open and willing to listen to your needs? Or a leader who just listens but dismisses it as soon as you've brought it up? Be a good listener, and not just listen for the sake of doing so. You need to be able to listen actively and really pay attention to what your team has to say and what they need from you. You are the one they will go to when they feel something needs to be improved. When your people know that their leader is taking their every concern seriously, no matter how small it may be, they will feel appreciated, and this will motivate them to perform better.

CHAPTER 3:

Why Diversity is Essential

*D*iversity is a subject that is not talked about enough at the workplace. The world is evolving rapidly, and yet, we're not embracing inclusion at the same pace. Diversity and discrimination are major issues that can cause a lot of problems at the workplace if they are not addressed adequately by the leaders. Why the leaders? Because the leaders are the ones who set the example for others to follow.

We're all different, and our differences can generate various points of view and contribute to creativity and innovation. Yet, many team leaders and businesses are not capitalising on this tremendous opportunity when they choose to either overlook or ignore the importance of diversity in today's work environment. In my time with top leaders, I have found that many fail to see that by embracing different talents, appreciating each member, and providing inclusive leadership, they can utilise the differences to achieve the overall goals and objectives better.

The Unspoken Problem

It's an unpleasant thing for an employee to feel like they don't belong. Our cities are changing. Our work environments and even the way we work is changing. But what's not changing is more diversity and inclusion. Men still <u>outnumber</u> women when it comes to leading organisations. In fact, in the United States alone, there are more men named John that are leaders of major companies than women leading major companies, according to one such <u>research</u>.

There is also another problem the workplace faces, and that is institutionalised racism. It is <u>well-documented</u> that if you have a name that sounds foreign, you have a harder time getting a job outside your country of origin. Yes, name discrimination exists, and it is a genuine, unspoken problem that nobody likes to talk about. It's there, and we're all feeling its impact and its presence, but nobody wants to address the issue directly.

Unconscious bias in the workplace is just that—*unconscious*. It occurs before we realise it, and it negatively shapes our judgement of people, especially when it comes to important decisions, like hiring, promoting, and developing talent. Due to its subtlety, unconscious bias leads to unintentional exclusion. But you can influence change by first recognising and acknowledging the importance of encouraging more diversity among your team.

As a leader, you have the unique opportunity to open yourself up to new ways of doing things to lead inclusively. Mentor someone different from you. Give an assignment to someone other than your average go-to person, perhaps. When promoting, think about who's made contributions that you've overlooked. Ask the shy or introverted employee for input during a meeting, get to know someone different from you by asking them to lunch, speak up when you hear inappropriate or disrespectful comments said in your presence. Don't assume the answer; ask questions to understand points of view that are different than yours. Monitor yourself and observe when your biases get in the way. There are so many things you could do to bring out change once you recognise the reason *why you need to encourage diversity*.

Not only is it the *right* thing to do, but also because from a strategic standpoint, it is one of the most *useful* things you can do. Boosting diversity in the company makes for a more successful company, and this is based on <u>studies</u> and <u>research</u>. For example, researchers at McKinsey found that racially diverse teams outperform the non-diverse teams by <u>35%</u>. We know that things need to change, but how do we go from talking about it actually to making it happen? Diversity is difficult. It takes resources, energy, and time; and companies don't always have the resources or time to address that. They need to be getting on with the other aspects of running a business and leading their teams.

Diversity is not being approached in the right way and with the right mindset. <u>Studies</u> show that forced diversity training could backfire negatively. It makes people feel resentful and increases prejudice. A lot of people suddenly think that if you're a minority or from a different background, you're getting opportunities handed to you not because you deserved them, but because a company was simply trying to fill its diversity quota. People are quick to attribute it to tokenism or diversity schemes, believing you only got that because you're a woman or from a different race. The problem is that institutionalised inequality is not being correctly addressed. The bad news is that there is no quick solution; there's no silver bullet. Addressing diversity takes time, and it takes effort. However, the good news is that the situation *can be changed*.

What Workplace Diversity Means

Workplace diversity happens when a company embraces a wide range of factors that make individuals unique. This includes culture, race, age, religion, gender, social status, personality, and even sexual orientation. It's more than just acknowledging the diversity of a population; it means appreciating all the things about a person that make them unique.

Why Does Diversity Matter?

Leaders need to make a commitment—a commitment to being consciously inclusive. A responsibility to respect differences, be accountable and embrace possibilities. Imagine the impact you can have if you chose to go with that approach. Diversity in the workplace promotes a positive working environment. An environment in which your employees will grow and thrive because no one feels excluded, left out, or out of place. When employees work with people from different backgrounds, they have a unique opportunity in their hands. They get the chance to learn from one another. In doing so, they are able to produce higher quality products and services.

Building a diverse team is important. No doubt, a varied group does come with its own set of challenges. But there is also a challenge to be found in a team that consists of all like-minded individuals. The scope of thinking is severely limited because when every person thinks of a problem in the same way as the others, no different solutions can be found. Diversity brings together many various aspects of society, race, gender, and background experiences, and includes them in one organisation. It is a strategy for better productivity and growth in the years ahead.

We live in an age where globalisation is on the rise, family structures are evolving and company structures are changing at an advanced pace. Diverse work environments are unavoidable, and some companies find themselves changing almost naturally to accommodate those needs. Employees can now work remotely, internationally, full-time or part-time, come from several generations, and more. Diversity in teams is a mixture; it comes with challenges but also benefits. Having a strong team of employees that have the opportunity to learn from different cultures, backgrounds and skillsets is one of those benefits. Becoming better collaborators and communicators is another. Problem-solving, a sharing of perspectives, there's a lot to be gained from incorporating diversity.

Expand Your Talent Pool

When you broaden your net, you get the best fish in the sea. A diverse talent pool means that employees from all different backgrounds, skillsets and experiences are coming together for a common goal. The team becomes *more well-rounded*, benefitting from these various perspectives, ideas, and inputs. Once your team sees that the organisation is a globally accepting firm, you will attract a diverse range of employees to work in your environment. This enables you with different perspectives and opportunities in the future, and equality in the workforce.

Bringing together all those different perspectives and skillsets can significantly catalyse your success rate. People *want* to work for your business when they realise it doesn't practice employment discrimination. It also helps with the retention of your current employees. They will want to stay at a company that promotes equality and is accepting of all backgrounds in an increasingly globalised economy.

It Promotes Innovation

Innovation comes from the conflicts that will undoubtedly arise when a team consists of a diverse background. But as you sit there and listen to various types of people with many different ideas, you will have the opportunity to create innovation for your products or services by *combining these ideas*. This encourages responsibility and emboldens the employee to contribute individually. New ideas are born, and the gaps in your business are filled. Your organisation thus gains a competitive advantage, leading to better market share and growth.

Your Customer Base Becomes Equally as Diverse

Showing that you understand diversity and, more importantly, *support* diversity, you will attract a different and equally diverse customer base, made up of different types of customers. More customers mean better business opportunities. This improves the reputation of your business. When your employees are thriving in their jobs, they will speak positively about your organisation, and word of mouth can be a very effective marketing approach to take.

By combining diverse cultures and experiences, you will have a broad understanding of what the consumer needs. Relationships within the community become widespread, because of the different language skills at play and the social awareness. Your connection with your clients is strengthened, and you show them that your business has many shared interests in common with them. It gives them something to relate to.

It Encourages Team Unity

By showing your team that your business is a source of acceptance to all differences, it makes them feel more trusted, respected, and those strong friendships will grow among the entire team. By developing their social skills, you motivate them always to give more. When your team sees that their leader and organisation value their unique and different traits, it encourages them to speak up with confidence and to perform their best. *Team morale* is given a boost as employees come together despite the differences in ideas and perspectives. The team and company culture improve, and you significantly increase your chances of retaining the best talents in the industry, especially among Millennials today who value workplace diversity.

Expanding Worldwide Becomes Easier

Being diverse means you're able to communicate well with people hailing from various parts of the world, which will dramatically increase your market share if you can win them over. A varied team knows how to form relationships and understand the nuances between different cultures, making it easier for your business to conquer the local markets in different regions.

Doing business abroad requires a thorough understanding of the local workforce. When you have team members who come from the country you're expanding to, the insight and knowledge that comes with it could be invaluable to your expansion. Diversity is crucial for an organisation's ability to innovate and adapt in a fast-changing environment. When you have variety in the workplace, your business is more open to the world and ready to grow.

A Boost in Creativity

With the different perspectives you gain in the team, *no stone is left unturned* when solutions are explored. Bouncing ideas off people who think and view the world differently from you can open your eyes to new possibilities and see things in a way you never have before. This, in turn, will encourage your team members to be more creative in their thinking and approach as they work together to figure out how to come up with the best possible solution.

A Team with a Dynamically Diverse Working Style

Keeping your team motivated, enthusiastic, and on their toes is easy when you bring together minds and personalities that think, act, and behave differently. Diversity *keeps things interesting* because you never know what new idea is going to come up next. As the leader, it allows you to watch how your team interacts with people of different backgrounds. And you'll be able to keep an eye out for the employee who displays the qualities of a potential leader in the making.

Diversity is beneficial. It's not about political correctness, and it's not about the mathematical proof for variety. In an advertising agency in London, a group of five creative directors got together and initiated the Great British Diversity Experiment. They enlisted 120 people who came from various backgrounds. They put these individuals into teams and asked these teams to problem-solve. The researchers studied them ethnographically, analysing them and observed the way they interacted in comparison to a homogenous group. They found that diverse groups were the more creative ones because they had access to more perspectives with all the different people involved. It makes you connect the dots in different ways. They issued a report at the end of the experiment, in that report, they said diversity is the new Darwinism. And this is absolutely right. The world is changing, and it always will keep changing as new things come up.

Companies must learn to evolve and change with the times, or risk going extinct.

The Challenges of a Diverse Workforce

As great as it is to see people from all walks of life come together to create, innovate, brainstorm, and share their unique perspectives while working together well as a team, diversity also comes with some challenges.

One problem with a diverse team is that some members may be native speakers of another language. They may not be bilingual and struggle to be well-versed in another. Not understanding each other's languages can lead to communication barriers and culture clashes, which are common when multiple cultures meet. This has a direct impact on the team's workflow and performance.

The problem with a too diverse team is that there's an increased tendency for employees to indulge in interpersonal conflicts. As different beliefs, values, traditions, norms and opinions come together, the chance of disagreements increase. This leads to the opportunity for employees to discuss work-unrelated topics, varying from serious to trivial reasons. Regardless of the cause, such conflicts result in the development of negative emotions in a team, slower decision making and lost productivity.

Another challenge is that people with different interests and values may struggle to connect. Without a common ground, it's not easy to start an exciting conversation, and therefore, it's hard to create a relationship. People don't work as good when they have no connection to the other team members, which will reflect in the overall performance.

The leader needs to cultivate a team that maximises benefits and overcomes challenges more than anything else. Instead of letting these challenges hold them back, leaders set the example of embracing diversity and encouraging their team to be comfortable with change. However, diversity can also backfire if the challenges become more of a hindrance than a help. That's why it's the leader's job to find the perfect balance between diversity and similarity.

How to Encourage Greater Diversity

Diversity is *everywhere*, in everything setting foundation and framework to our lives. It can be found in the food we eat, the clothes we wear, the activities we want to do each day (because doing the same thing repeatedly is going to become dull and mundane), the groups of people we choose to spend our time with. Diversity is even found in the animal kingdom among the different species and subspecies. So why not encourage more of this at the workplace too? Canadian Prime Minister Justin Trudeau knocked it out of the park when he put together a diverse team as part of his Cabinet. In doing so, he achieved diversity, inclusion, and equality. All decisions that are going to be made now, and in the future, will be a reflection of those different minds coming together.

The time for change is always now. Not tomorrow, not next week, next month, or a year from now, it's *now*. We shouldn't wait for the "right time" to make a move for the better, we should seize the day and the opportunity when it comes. There is a lot that can be done as a team, a leader, and an organisation as a whole. For example, if you're handling the recruitment process, consider ways that you can minimise your unconscious bias. In the 1970s and 1980s, the symphony orchestra in the United States, was made up of all white men. They decided to hold blind auditions to do something about that. Musicians auditioned behind the screen so the person in charge of hiring couldn't tell if it was a man or woman, what the colour of their skin was. The result of this approach was that the number of women getting accepted into orchestras increased between 25 to 46%.

Another company, called GapJumpers, took this idea of blind auditions and applied it to the corporate world. Instead of looking through CVs to screen their candidates, they assigned challenges anonymously. As a result, there were 60% more minority applicants selected for interviews. Suddenly, it's no longer a question of not being able to find the "best candidate" after all. The problem was the best candidates were often overlooked due to unconscious bias.

An example of what can be done to address the issue of diversity is to say something, even if nobody says anything. Nothing changes if we all keep silent. So if you are in a room, in a meeting, in a company, talk to your leader and co-workers. Talk about diversity and inclusion, show that you're aware of what's going on.

A great team leader leverages the strengths of its members and uses those strengths to offset any weaknesses. The leader knows that an employee is so much more than just the job that they're doing. They are unique, interesting individuals with their own set of talents, skills, and knowledge that open you up to a wealth of new opportunities. Let go of the emotions and preconceived notions or judgments that impede your progress, and embrace the feelings that will bring you several steps forward.

In your role as a leader, the way to encourage greater diversity in a work environment is to:

- Challenge yourself
- Encourage a culture of openness
- Highlight diversity
- Work on improving your social skills

- Keep an open mind and listen with one too
- Encourage team empathy
- Remove the barriers
- Allow flexible work hours
- Ensure social activities are inclusive

The most important part of the content I share here is you. Be sure to integrate this continually and with each new idea—how would I do that? Would they believe me if I tried that? Which projects would this work for? Don't just read these concepts without engaging with the ideas, always think of ways to implement these strategies.

Challenge Yourself

Instead of looking at the common ground among your employees, *start looking for the differences*. Focus on that during your thought process and encourage your team to reflect on what they appreciate most about working with someone who is from a different background than they are.

For example, when you're working together on a project with your team; at the start of the project, encourage them to share about what they think makes them different and how this strength can benefit the outcome of the project. This is also an opportunity for you, the leader, to observe whether there is too much of the same kind of thinking taking place because you subconsciously put together a team of people who thought the same way you did. If that's the case, then this is your opportunity to take corrective action by including more diversity moving forward.

The first step in addressing a problem that needs to be fixed is first to acknowledge that *there is a problem.*

Encourage a Culture of Cohesiveness

When employees feel like they might be the odd one out, they think they don't belong and will not have the confidence to speak up and share their ideas. The leader's responsibility is to *encourage openness* so plans can be discussed freely. For this to happen, respect is one of the major key principles that absolutely must be present. An effective leader consistently inspires and helps their people overcome challenges faced without depreciating them. They are ones that provide a work environment where employees help each other and value the contributions that everyone makes.

Highlight Diversity

Talk about it, mention it in the job ads that you post when recruiting potential new employees, encourage your team to refer to other potential employees from groups that may be underrepresented and reward them for it. During the interview process, have a diverse panel for greater equality and fairness. Create policies at work that are diversity-friendly and reassess the current employee benefits in place to ensure parity across all groups.

Work on Improving Your Social Skills

Communication skills promote cultural diversity. Today's workplace is a melting pot of diverse cultures and languages. For everyone to be able work in harmony, it is crucial to have good social skills handy.

A leader should encourage the team as a whole to work on improving their social skills too. Social skills lend to a strong social presence, and in the career world where connections and networking matter, *being able to socialise is an invaluable resource*. It makes it easier to build teams that are productive and cohesive, who work well together to get things done.

Social skills help you maintain positive and amicable relationships with your co-workers, regardless of how different your backgrounds may be. You are going to spend most of your day working together with them, and without the proper social skills on hand, it can be difficult to build and construct productive relationships. (more about social skills in chapter 5)

Keep an Open Mind and Listen with One Too

Listen with an open mind, and you'll be more receptive to what you're hearing. Being judgmental or opinionated can disrupt your efforts to encourage unity and harmony among your followers. Judgement is a poor use of time that distracts and weakens our focus.

The minute you start getting distracted with your own thoughts, your active listening abilities are compromised, and you won't be as receptive to new ideas as you should be. *Everyone has a story to tell*, and there is always something you can learn from someone who is different from you. Encourage open-mindedness and the willingness to listen receptively among your team by demonstrating your desire to do the same. Lead by example.

Encourage Team Empathy

Encourage the entire team to put themselves in their colleague's shoes and try to feel every emotion that they do. The joy, sadness, distress, frustration, happiness, anger, whatever it is they may be feeling, especially if they are new to the team and trying to find a way to fit in. Sometimes we forget that the ones who seem on the outs are struggling and trying their best to fit in, and it's much harder to do when they don't feel welcomed by their team. It can be a very demoralising and unhappy experience.

Through empathy, your listening abilities improve because you immerse yourself in the world of another. You start to pay a little bit more attention to the way someone else feels. This skill is at the core of what it means to be a great leader and listener; someone people love talking and pouring their hearts out to. Being empathic needs focus and concentration, but the effort that gets put in will be worth it when you see how well your team comes together as soon as more empathy is at play.

Remove the Barriers

Strive to remove all barriers, especially those that restrict the disabled from *being able to perform to their fullest potential*. For example, someone with a visual impairment might not be able to use a mouse properly on the computer. What they would do instead is use the "Tab" key to navigate through a document. They would also use a screen reader to read the content aloud, but for this to work, the texts need to be correctly formatted with headings, subheadings, and so on. This approach to formatting documents is actually good practice since it makes the content easy to understand for anyone who is using it, including the customers. Passageways in the building should also be kept clear, enabling those with physical disabilities to move about more freely. Installing equipment like induction loops for those with cochlear implants or hearing aids is another example of how to encourage inclusiveness.

Allow Flexible Work Hours

The ability to work from home, have flexible work hours, or job sharing can be the difference between having to give up their job or being able to continue contributing their skills to the team. This is especially true if they have other commitments they're trying to balance with work. As long as your employee is getting the job done, it doesn't matter if they are physically in the office or not. It matters whether you can *count on them and trust them*. Flexible work environments make it easier for employees who have had to go on an extended break, like maternity leave, for example, to ease back into the work structure.

Ensure Social Activities Are Inclusive

Some activities organised by the company might not be suitable for all employees. For instance, holding a team get-together session over dinner and drinks is not going to be the best activity for an employee who may be a recovering alcoholic, someone on medication, or someone who needs to drive quite a distance to get back home. Consider more inclusive alternatives when planning office and team after-work activities. Of course, that is not to say that a group of friends can't go out after work and enjoy a few drinks together. Rather, this is about ensuring that the activities planned are thought of with everyone in mind, not just a selected group of individuals.

Employees who work and play together, stay together as a team. *Bonding with your team outside of work* is an important relationship-building exercise. It helps everyone to enjoy each other's company without thinking about work for a change, and that bond of friendship will carry over and fuel their motivation when it's crunch time again. Plan activities that ensure no one in your team is excluded because of a personal situation.

Before you start turning all concepts of your organisation upside down, you need to remember that having a too diverse team could be detrimental. The most important aspect of teamwork is that your team members can enjoy working together, and if people don't get along well, it's hard to create something collectively. Nevertheless, don't get encouraged by that because as we've seen, having different viewpoints and opinions may lead to conflicts, but the outcome will be all the better. The key is to start being more aware of diversity, then slowly implementing it into your team dynamic and *finding the perfect balance*, so you don't destroy what's already built.

CHAPTER 4:

Is Your Team Having Fun?

$\mathcal{G}$rowing and nurturing a diverse team is going to be a new experience for many leaders. While you're focused on efficiency and ensuring that everyone on the team is getting along well and doing what they are supposed to, there's another vital aspect you need to pay attention to: *Are they having fun?*

It's a common misconception that "having fun at work" means the employees are slacking off and not doing their duties, but it is important to note that fun can come in several forms. The old perception of "having fun" should be dismissed, because enjoying a day at work does not mean that responsibilities are being neglected. A good team leader knows it is imperative to create the workday as engaging as possible, so the employees don't feel that the day is dragging by. People should actually enjoy coming into the office and avoid the dreaded *Sunday Gloom* when they know Monday is approaching.

When It's All Work and No Play

Everyone knows at least one person who dreads going into work and hates their job. They're miserable and frequently complain about how much they hate being at the office and can't wait for the day when they get to leave. If it isn't them who hates their job, it's their colleague at the office who looks unhappy as they're typing away behind the desk. They come to work, clock in, and clock out for the sake of taking home a paycheck, and that's about it. There's no joy, no motivation, no passion, and worst of all, not an ounce of happiness. Coming to work for them almost feels like a prison sentence, something they are forced to do because they have to earn a living. Maybe at some point, you were feeling that way before you found yourself in the leadership position. There are several reasons why employees could be feeling this way, they are:

- There's no entertainment value, and they don't enjoy what they're doing.
- There's no element of play or fun in the tasks that they have to handle.
- They're stressed.
- They don't feel supported.
- They don't feel like they have any connections or good relationships with anyone at the office.
- They're not living up to their full potential.
- They don't see a goal or vision of the direction they're going.
- They don't see any room for growth in their current organisation.

Considering that about <u>one-third</u> of an employee's life is spent at work, that's a lot of time to spend unhappy. *90,000* hours of your life are spent at your job, and if you don't enjoy what you do, you're going to spend a third of your life feeling miserable and dreading every single minute.

Employees feel disengaged and demotivated at work when they don't feel challenged enough. Yes, it isn't *fun* that is going to make them slack off, it's *not being challenged*. When they don't feel challenged, they can become bored, disengaged, and even complacent. However, feeling overwhelmed could also cause them to feel miserable. Perhaps they are the star playing on their team, and their managers and leaders keep piling the work on, thinking they can handle it and not realising the employee is starting to feel overwhelmed but not saying anything about it. This can result in stress, anxiety, and irritability, feeling like they never have enough time in the day to get the job done.

Almost every leader or manager has experienced that dreaded moment when an employee asks to speak to them privately. They walk into the office, and once the doors are shut, that's when the employee hands in their letter of resignation. More than once, the leader has found themselves feeling taken aback or even shocked, especially when the letter happens to come from one of their best employees. They never realised there was a problem and the resignation has taken them completely by surprise.

They didn't see this move coming at all and ask the employee, *"Why are you leaving? Were you not happy here?"* The leader or manager might even start to question themselves, wondering what they could have done better or whether *they* are the cause the employee is leaving. Unfortunately, that's a case of too little too late.

Here's the thing, the reason your employee is going to give you as to why they are leaving is *not going to be the truth*. They're still going to keep it polite and professional, citing by-the-book reasons. They're too afraid of burning bridges, and that fear is enough to squash any desire they have to be honest and share the truth. They're not going to tell you outright that they're leaving because of their tedious work and the demotivation. *They're not going to tell you that they're leaving because they are not having fun,* although that is one of the key points that factored into their decision.

Not having fun at work is one of the reasons why many companies are *losing good employees*. They're not enjoying themselves because they're not working in projects that energise them. Every once in a while, we all have to do tasks that we don't necessarily like, even leaders. You might hate talking on the phone, but if your job requires you to speak to a client now and then, it's not the end of the world. However, when an employee finds themselves spending all of their time doing things that they hate, the balance is clearly off. This is where leaders run into problems and must quickly think about how to manage the employee's emotions before they call it quits completely.

The Dreaded Stress Factor

When an employee doesn't love what they do, just the thought of having to go to work is enough to start triggering the dreaded stress factor. Globally, feeling stressed in the workplace is on the rise. Employees in China have the highest level of workplace stress, at a staggering 86%, while 91% of Australians adults report that they feel stressed in at least one major area of their lives. 25% of employees say that their job is the number one stress factor in their lives. 29% of employees feel quite a bit or extremely stressed when they're at work.

What's worse, job stress is the biggest <u>reason</u> behind why so many employees today fall sick, call in sick, and experience financial or personal problems. The dreaded stress factor is unavoidable if your employees are not enjoying themselves. When you love what you do, somehow, everything still feels manageable. Yes, the stress is still there, but you're not focused on the negative aspects of your job because you love what you do, and that passion for the job is enough to get you through it.

It is not uncommon for employees to experience some form of stress-related anxiety or depression in their jobs, an unspoken side effect of what happens when the fun is severely lacking in the environment. Unfortunately, those types of work conditions are more common than a work environment where leaders understand the importance of making sure that the employees are enjoying their time at work. A lot of leaders are still stuck in that mindset where fun means work is not getting done, and people are slacking off. They're stuck in that mindset of "you're not paid to have fun, you're paid to work," not realising that the cost of that attitude and mentality is causing the stress they are inflicting on their employees, stress that is counterproductive.

Many bosses are so worried about employees having too much fun at work and not performing their duties that they fail to recognise a stressed-out employee *cannot* perform their duties well either. Stress is a genuine problem at work, especially when you consider one report that indicated 25% of employees feel like screaming out loud when they're at work because of stress. Another 14% secretly harboured the desire to punch their colleagues in the face. This is not something you want to experience when you're trying to manage a team of effective, productive employees the way you envisioned.

The real problem here is that stress is being overlooked in favour of "getting the job done," and it is the employees who are paying the price for it. Stress is a silent killer, and nowhere is this more evident than when we are overworked. Being overworked can affect you significantly, both mentally and physically. We may not feel it while we're working, but when it hits you, it hits hard. One day you wake up and realise you're completely exhausted and burned out because you've been overworked for far too long.

The environment you spend the most time in is going to have the biggest influence on your psyche. For most employees, that's their workplace. If you're constantly in a fast-paced, high-pressured, on-the-go stressful environment, it is likely to be one of your triggers. There's a lot that could be contributing to your stress: a manager that is breathing down your neck over the deadline that is looming, a heavy workload, struggling to build bonds and connections with your colleagues because you feel like you're the odd one out. It's hard to think clearly. You're feeling scattered and forgetful. Every day feels like another day of misery where nothing seems to go right. Studies show that those who reportedly undergo a lot of stress feel tired all the time and less productive as their day progresses. These are all genuine consequences of what happens when the fun-factor at work is overlooked in favour of getting the job done.

What makes the job of the leader even more challenging when managing a team of diverse employees is that everyone experiences stress very differently. The way one person responds or reacts to the situation probably won't be the same as another person's. One person might struggle when they are under pressure, while another might thrive. This makes it even more difficult to identify when an employee might be feeling too much pressure, even more so since they're unlikely to come to you about it and tell you outright, *"I'm feeling stressed at my job."*

Our bodies were not built to cope with it, and once it reaches the chronic stage, it might be too late if the damaging effects inflicted are already permanent. The problem is we live in a society that has conditioned us to believe that we need to do more in less time, and poor mental health is the price to be paid. When an employee is feeling stressed at work, they will never be able to live up to their full potential.

Having fun at work is no longer an option. *It's a necessity* if you want a team that is performing, motivated, and able to work together as a unit despite the diversity. This way, you will retain your top performers, increase productivity and build overall team strength. It is the leader's role to ensure that your team is engaged and enjoying themselves *without* them having to ask you to do it.

Your team is not going to speak up and tell you they need more fun or that they're feeling stressed. They're not going to speak up because they're not sure if you're going to support them, stigmatise them, or manage them right out of the role, and they're not willing to risk that. Even when you tell them to feel free to come to you with a problem, they're going to be hesitant about it. Your employee *wants* to be at work and do their best, but they can't be at their best if they're not enjoying themselves, plain and simple. Don't wait until it's past the breaking point or for something to happen before you say, *"I should have done this."* By then it's usually too late. No, ensuring that your team is having fun begins from the moment you step into your role as a leader, and it never stops.

The Importance of Having Fun

The idea of having fun at work needs to be redefined. It's not about hanging around in the break room, sipping coffee, talking, and idling your time away. Having fun at work is about work-life balance, the friendships you make, not having to stress unnecessarily, *looking forward* to coming to work instead of dreading it. *That's fun at work*. If your team is not having fun at work, who's going to want to come to work?

The human brain has a circuit found in the areas of the brain that store and process emotions involving playfulness. In fact, to play promotes the plasticity of the brain, helping you feel young and happy. It engages the creative areas of the brain, something a company can benefit from since creativity leads to better solutions. The mistake that most companies are currently making is to separate work from play when what they should be doing instead is bringing the personal joy of playfulness into the work experience. It may not sound like the conventional image we have associated with what work should be about, but neurologically and emotionally, it's going to be the best approach to take for the sake of your team's long-term happiness.

An affirmative leader understands that a group that enjoys having a good time together is *not wasting time*. They're creating a bond without trying too hard, and that relationship is going to carry into the work that they have to do together. A team that likes each other performs significantly better than a unit that rubs each other the wrong way or doesn't get along. Having fun as a team builds social and emotional capital, which simultaneously minimises stress and improves their performance at a task.

No one was such a firm believer in using levity to drive productivity as Herb Kelleher, the former CEO of Southwest Airlines. His philosophy was so good that he never had to force anyone to go along with his ideas. Instead, he incorporated an element of fun to drive his initiatives, which were extremely successful and that's why he is still remembered fondly as a beloved leader.

Kelleher once settled a legal suit with an arm-wrestling match, and on several occasions, he used to dress up as Elvis Presley or a rabbit. Why? To keep his employees happy and smiling, that's why. Under Kelleher's leadership, Southwest Airlines built a reputation as one of the nation's most profitable airlines, proof that fun at the office is not a waste of time after all. Having fun encourages employees to think outside the box because a team that regularly spends time together having fun will eventually be comfortable enough around each other to let their guard down. When the emotional walls are down and the team is at ease, they're not afraid to speak their mind and bounce ideas back and forth, no matter how impossible or outrageous those ideas may seem. When this level of comfort is present among the team, that's when they generate some of their best and most innovative ideas and solutions.

A work environment that values fun as much as it values hard work is critical in retaining current employees and just as crucial toward attracting new employees. Nobody wants to work for a company that is negative, miserable, and nothing but toxic. Everyone wants to work at a fun company. Fun should not be relegated to the bottom of your priority list. As the leader, you need to be an enabler and allow the fun to thrive in your team. Permit your employees to be human. Be open to giving and receiving fun and humour at the workplace.

No matter how diverse and different in personality your team may be, if they're enjoying themselves, they're communicating better, and they're building trust and friendships. When your people are having fun, they're working harder and they're managing their stress better. Want to be a great leader and be remembered as a legend the way <u>Kelleher</u> was? Then fun might be what you need more of in the workplace.

How Do I Tell If My Team Is Enjoying Themselves?

Take a good look at the productivity levels among your team right now. How much work get they done? Are they meeting the deadlines? Observe their body language when they walk in the door every morning and throughout the day at work. Do they have a smile on their face, stand up tall, make eye contact, look animated, and engaged in the conversations they have? Or are their shoulders hunched from the invisible burden of stress that they're carrying around with them? Do they look tired? Out of sorts? Do they have a smile that doesn't quite reach their eyes and somehow looks forced?

Communication goes far beyond verbal abilities. Some of the most powerful forms of communication come in the form of body language. While the mouth can tell a lie, body language is far more revealing; what is said in those unspoken and nonverbal cues will show how that person really is feeling. Your team is not going to tell you outright that they're unhappy, even when you ask them, they're going to say everything is alright or okay. But their body language is going to tell a different story.

Your people *need* work-life balance to maintain their happiness and their motivation. They need to take care of themselves to avoid doing too much too soon and burning out quickly, especially when they don't enjoy the work they've been assigned (not every task is going to be enjoyable). That kind of work style can never be sustained for long, and it will eventually rob your team of happiness and motivation to do anything. Use appraisals or quarterly review sessions as a time to catch up and encourage them to be honest with you about what may be weighing on their mind. Make a conscious effort to pay close attention to the body language of a person, a skill that is especially useful when conducting face-to-face sessions. Better yet, get the team together to brainstorm how everyone thinks they could be having more fun at work.

Striking a Balance between Work and Play

Striking this balance begins with a shift in the mindset of the leader. To move away from the mentality of "play" equals work not getting done is the very first and most crucial step in this process. Move away from that mindset and towards "better work-life balance" thinking. This is what your employees are in dire need of—a *balance* between their work and their play.

What does work-life balance look like? Well, for one thing, you could begin to encourage your employees not to take their work home with them. That would be a great place to start. Encourage them to break the habit of bringing work home with them (if that is what they've been doing) and tell them there's *no reason* they should feel guilty about it. Remind them that they've already put in 7 to 8 hours of their time during the day to commit to their job, now it's time to use the rest of the day for themselves.

Another example of how to encourage a more pleasant and enjoyable work environment is to reduce the stress your team feels in terms of work—for example, learning to say "no" when they've already got too much on their plate to juggle. This is a major one and probably the hardest for most people to do. Saying "no" can often induce a lot of feelings of guilt, especially when they are worried their job or reputation might be at risk. When talking to your team about a task, let them know you would like them to take it on, but if it is too much, it's okay for them to say no. Highlight that they should not feel guilty about this, and about how saying no is an essential time-management skill if they want to put a stop to being perpetually overcommitted and stressed.

When your team feels they have the support of their leader and the ability to say no if they think they're unable to commit to something, they'll be a lot happier because you gave them that choice. Flexibility is an attractive quality to many employees, especially with the modern mindset today that is starting to prioritise work-life balance. With a better work-life balance and decreased stress levels, employees are less likely to fall sick.

Celebrating the Little Victories

Too often a team gets caught up in the bigger goal that they forget to celebrate the little wins and victories along the way. Working toward a big goal is a massive undertaking, and small celebrations in between help remind your team about how far they have come and the remarkable progress they have made working together. This keeps the employees motivated to keep going when they can see themselves moving forward, and they'll be fired up to work much harder to achieve the next milestone. Encourage your team to set their own milestones and decide what the celebration should be to lift their spirits.

Introducing Super Casual Fridays

Ring in the weekend early at work by going beyond the regular "jeans and t-shirt" dress code by taking casual Friday's a step further. Organise team lunches every Friday, or end work an hour early so your team can go home and be with their families for the weekend.

A Little Friendly Competition

A little friendly competition with prizes involved is a great way to lighten the mood around the office. Organise something mid-week to break the monotony or plan a friendly competition once a month. Get your team to throw out ideas about what they would like the prizes to be, so you're actually giving them something to be excited about.

A Social Network of Your Own

Technology makes almost anything possible, even the ability to create a private social network just for your team. *Yammer* is an example of a service that helps you quickly and easily set up a social network at work. The employees can collaborate, post funny content they came across online, and stay up to date on what's happening in the lives of their colleagues, like if a special occasion or a birthday is coming up.

Commit to One Day of "Fun at Work"

The "Fun at Work Day" is one day each month, where the focus is geared toward fun instead of work. Instead of asking them to give up their weekends to attend team-building retreats, make Fun at Work Day happen on a workday. Let it be a day filled with games, team building activities, lunch and tea-time get together sessions, bring your pet to work, taking longer lunch breaks, and watching a movie at the office as you bond over food and drinks. Don't think of this as a day of work wasted, because the boost of happiness that your employees are going to get out of this one day will more than make up for it because their productivity levels will soar sky-high when they come into work tomorrow. It will give them something to work hard for and look forward to every month.

CHAPTER 5:

The Secrets of Communication, EQ, and Vulnerability

E mbracing diversity, encouraging fun, motivation, happiness, and productivity, there are so many aspects of successfully leading a team. Having your attention pulled in different directions, it can be easy to forget to focus on the finer subtleties of building the strong characteristics you need as the leader of a team.

One such finer nuance is the emotional intelligence (EQ) aspect. We are all highly emotional creatures (by nature), and over the last few years, the importance of emotional intelligence has been brought to the forefront. We should recognise and understand the importance of having the freedom to be openly expressive with our emotions.

A powerful team consists of individuals with a heightened focus upon their emotional intelligence and who are willing to communicate with one another, even in the most vulnerable of times. In my experience, this open line of communication has been immensely helpful in encouraging work to flow much better among a diverse team and leave each member feeling confident and empowered enough to speak their mind. Emotional intelligence is the next secret ingredient that is needed to remove resistance and generate a positive environment which can bring productive change.

Most people are afraid to talk about their emotions. Emotions have a bad connotation associated with them. Society has conditioned us to believe that showing emotions is a sign of weakness—a lack of control. We're taught to keep our chin up and have a stiff upper lip, presenting a strong facade even though that's far from what we may be feeling on the inside. Never let them see you cry or be emotional. This negative connotation associated with emotions is the reason why emotional intelligence was never given much focus in the past, until now.

What Does It Mean to Be Emotionally Intelligent?

It is crucial to distinguish the difference between emotions and the value that *emotional intelligence* has. Emotional intelligence, commonly referred to as EQ, is something fundamentally different. EQ is the ability to identify and manage *your emotions* and the emotions of *others*. It is possible to increase your EQ, and that's why we take a closer look at it right now.

EQ calls for emotional awareness, having empathy towards yourself and others. It also calls for the ability to harness your emotions and apply them to tasks like thinking or problem-solving. It requires the ability to manage emotions, and this includes regulating your own feelings and the emotions of the people around you. If someone needs to be calmed down, the high EQ leader would know what to do and how to do it effectively. If someone needs cheering up, the EQ leader knows how to make them feel better. Emotions are responsible for some of the best and worst moments in our lives. Emotions are the reason why love feels so incredible, yet they are also the reason why breakups feel so terrible. They are the reason why getting a promotion at work makes you feel jubilant, and at the same time, they are responsible for the misery and unhappiness you feel if you lose your job.

Being very emotional does not automatically mean you have a high level of EQ, because you may be displaying your emotions freely. *Still, you're not thinking about your emotions or why you have them.* That's the difference. You might not even be considering the appropriateness of showing these emotions in certain situations. The problem is we're not taught the value of emotions in school as we were growing up. If your family members didn't understand the importance of EQ or practiced it themselves, then chances are you were probably not exposed to this much either. Children and teenagers often struggle to contain their emotions, and emotions hit them hard because they can neither fully understand their feelings or those of others.

When we're experiencing a negative emotion, our first thought is often *"there must be something wrong with me,"* or *"I'm not supposed to be feeling this way."* People judge, bully each other, get stuck in toxic friendships and relationships, and hurt each other. Why? All due to insecurity and a lack of emotional intelligence. It's hard to differentiate between yourself and someone else, and it's even more challenging to connect on an emotional level. To change that and truly comprehend where someone else is coming from, we have to consider emotional intelligence as a significant skill in our society. We must take the time to work on it consciously. Currently, most leaders do neither. Getting the chance to know yourself, to connect with yourself and your emotions are a fundamental part of being emotionally intelligent.

The Difference Between EQ and IQ

Daniel Goleman's emotional intelligence model is probably the most talked about and referred to today. Mention emotional intelligence and those who are already familiar with its concepts will instantly recognise Goleman's name (author of the bestselling book *Emotional Intelligence*). Goleman's work on emotional intelligence is linked closely to management and leadership abilities, and he states that EQ comprises five main components, or what he refers to as *"pillars of emotional intelligence."*

The first is *self-awareness,* which is a person's ability to be aware of their own emotions and be acutely aware of how these emotions affected them. It's the start of developing high EQ.

The second is *self-regulation*, which focuses on how well you can manage your emotions and predict the effects they will have. This is only possible if you're aware of your emotions (first pillar) and make it a habit of questioning them.

The third pillar is *motivation,* which is a big part of emotional intelligence. It is responsible for success because it keeps your drive going. Without emotional intelligence, it would be very easy to give in to your desire to quit or run away when things become difficult.

The fourth is *empathy,* because, in everything that you do in your life, people will be affected. Work, family, social settings, everything involves coming into contact with other people, which is why you must go the extra mile to understand the people around you and build meaningful connections.

The fifth and final pillar is *social skills;* they are the reason a person can become successful. Through social skills, you learn to become a better leader, someone who makes a difference in the lives of others. Someone who can manage conflicts and efficiently resolve them. You understand how to effectively maintain your interpersonal relationships so you can elicit the response you need from the people around you.

IQ, on the other hand, is more about pattern recognition, reasoning and logical problem-solving. Goleman then believes that EQ is not that much different from IQ. The quality that differentiates these two traits is that EQ is focused on how smart you are in the way that you interact with your own emotions and with other people. It is not merely about communicating with the people around you, but how effectively you interact with them.

At work, you can see first-hand why the importance of EQ over IQ is apparent. Although IQ as is certainly one of the main ingredients towards achieving success, EQ is a trait that many businesses will look for in a potential leader first. This is because a leader's primary job would be to lead the people around them. They need to inspire others, to get their teams working well together in a cohesive and unified manner, to be able to manage conflict when it arises. All of these skills require that the leader is able to gauge the emotions and read the people around them. It is EQ that helps leaders distinguish and identify what an employee's strengths and weaknesses are, not IQ. It is EQ that will enable leaders to get along well with various groups of individuals, not IQ. To possess great social skills and to help you excel with the clients, you need a high EQ, not IQ.

Despite their differences, both EQ and IQ are important traits and ideally should be used to maximise your strengths, although EQ is, without a doubt, the feature which is much more important to succeed both in life and the workplace.

Do We Need Emotions in a Team?

Yes, we do. It's scientifically proven that humans make decisions based on their emotions. That's why you need to acknowledge your and the emotions of others, so you understand the decision-making process in every situation. Emotions also help us understand the people around us based on the way we express ourselves through facial expression and body language. It clues someone else in as to how you may be feeling. It is through the emotions we express that others might get important clues or indicators as to how they should act next.

Emotional intelligence is not a skill that is meant for the leader alone. It is intended for *everyone* in the team. The emotional cues and signals we decipher can lead to a wealth of information. Since social communication is a big part of how we develop meaningful relationships, understanding emotional cues allows us to react and respond appropriately. Being a leader means you're going to have to influence the people around you to some degree, and that requires an "emotional" touch. This is a crucial step in the process because, without it, you wouldn't be able to inspire enough confidence in others, for them to follow your lead.

The way a leader acts has a profound influence on the group and vice versa. A charismatic leader can inspire great change and have a positive effect on the people. Ultimately, it leads to much better teamwork when we learn that empathy and understanding can go a long way. Our emotions construct a big part of who we are. We may try to hide it, ignore it, live in denial about it, but emotions are essentially what makes us so wonderfully, beautifully human.

Today, emotional intelligence has become a necessity. Why? Because you are more likely to fall into negative behaviour patterns when you don't have a high-level EQ guiding the way. A prime example would be a time when you handled a situation poorly, and it ended up costing you a great deal. You regret the way that you managed things at the time, and if you could turn back the clock, you would do it so much better. Dwelling on this negative experience only makes matters worse. Think of what the compounding effect would be if you reacted negatively and poorly in almost every situation you ever dealt with. Things will only get worse for you, and you'll become more frustrated and pessimistic with your life because it feels like nothing ever goes right. You can sometimes see the effects of what happens when people don't know what to do with their emotions; they become anxious, depressed, demoralised, withdrawn, anti-social, have numerous social problems, become problematic, and more. Don't go this path, understand your emotions and how to react to them.

The Emotionally Intelligent Leader

EQ means knowing who you are and being the role model that your team needs. EQ is a skill that needs to be learned, and like every other new skill you set out to learn, it starts with understanding which areas you need to improve. You want to be able to master these skills to a point where you're no longer actively thinking about it; you just do it like driving a car. That's called unconscious competence, and like learning how to drive, EQ needs practice, *a lot* of practice until you have mastered the way it works. Everything is difficult before it gets easy. In the beginning it's difficult because you're going to have to put in conscious effort thinking about it all the time and expending all your mental energy focusing on getting it right, but after a while it'll become easier.

Leading a team without understanding its emotions is like driving a car without knowing how to change gears (and no, it's not an automatic one). In the past, the leader was the one deciding the direction. All the people were simply following his or her lead. All the teams were following in the leader's footsteps. Leadership is no longer like that. It is now about creating connections and creating relationships, so you need to be able to manage emotions in this new kind of environment. To become the emotionally intelligent leader capable of leading your team to great success, multiple things must be done.

Acknowledge Emotions

Antonio Damasio's research revealed that those who experienced damage in the part of the brain that dealt with emotions found themselves having a much harder time making rational decisions. Damasio talked about his patient named Elliot, who had a brain cancer removed, along with the damaged part of the frontal lobe of Elliot's brain that was affected by the tumour. After the surgery, Elliot experienced a shift in his decision-making abilities. His ability to plan for the future and make decisions seemed to have weakened. Damasio wrote in his words: *"Elliot appears to be a man with normal intellect who was unable to decide properly, especially when the decisions involved personal or social matters."* We make decisions based on our feelings; that's how important emotions are to us.

The first small but simple step you can take to improve is to acknowledge emotions. Instead of denying them, try observing them with a curious mind. Ask people with genuine interest how they are feeling. When *you* are asked how you're feeling, answer with authenticity. Also, tell your team to do the same. Instead of complaining about their colleagues behind their back, encourage them to talk about the way they feel.

Erase the Taboo

When your team talks about or reveals their emotions, tell them it's okay to do so. Reassure them that emotions are not something to feel guilty over, but rather something that can be learned from. Instead of being afraid to address emotions, *embrace talking about it openly*. People who are interested, willing to learn and improve have what it takes to become successful. You can set an example by erasing the taboo that exists in our society when it comes to talking about emotions because this taboo is what's stopping all of us from taking the next step.

Reflect on the Origin of That Emotion

Knowing why we experience a particular emotion helps us deal with and process our feelings. It gives us time to actively reflect on how these emotions make us feel mentally and physically. It also gives us time to think about what triggered the emotion, and with these details, we can think about how to handle it better, moving forward.

Analysing and Accepting Emotions

Sometimes, when we express a feeling, we substitute one word for a word that we are more familiar with or better able to accept. In doing so, we're not accurately describing the emotion. However, there are a lot of distinctive emotions, each with a specific function. Every emotion has a different way it should be handled, and therefore, it's important to get to the root cause of the feeling. Accept and appreciate all those emotions because they are neither good nor bad. It's *the way that we handle them* that makes a difference. Grieving or sadness, for example, why are we so desperately trying to cut it out of our lives? To pretend we're okay rather than embrace how we feel? In truth, grief and sadness can be a beautiful illustration of the appreciation that we have for someone or something.

Ask Your Team Questions

Ask your team, *"How do you feel about...?"* A leader cannot manage the energy of a team if they don't know how they think about goals, about new challenges, about the way they feel about their team, or about new colleagues at work. It's crucial to ask your colleagues for their opinion so that you can adjust the necessary things and improve the work environment.

Learning to Listen Better

Learn how to be present in a conversation and how to share your feelings when you talk to your team. People have great ideas, and if you take the time to listen and let them get their point across, you're *demonstrating respect* for their opinions. This, in turn, makes them feel comfortable about opening up to you, which then allows you to regulate their emotions effectively. This use of emotional intelligence eventually leads to better teamwork and increased productivity all around while allowing you to demonstrate the abilities of a leader.

As soon as you master your emotions, and in the process get better at it, you will find it easier and easier to handle the emotions of others. Becoming an emotionally intelligent leader is a journey that begins by simply asking a person how you can support them. If we were all emotionally intelligent, what a difference would it make in the way we address variation? Or how would we approach topics like mental health? Imagine the world that we would be living in. An environment full of mutual understanding, acceptance, tolerance, and connection. A truly inclusive world. Now wouldn't that be something?

Building Your Emotionally Intelligent Team

An effective leader uses EQ skills to influence and persuade others under their leadership to pursue and work together towards a common goal. In an organisation, productivity levels run higher when a leader with high EQ is present. These leaders are the driving force behind the collective success of a group.

It was a group effort, but the one who inspired the achievement behind the scenes was the EQ leader. And the way to do this is by building an emotionally intelligent team.

Vanessa Urch Druskat and Steven B. Wolff, the people behind the *Building the Emotional Intelligence of Groups* research findings affirm that emotional intelligence skills were the underlying principle upon which successful teams were effectively built. EQ makes you (and every employee) a better team player with a greater capacity to genuinely connect on a deep and meaningful level with the team. Hard conversations become easier when empathy, self-awareness, and social skills are present. Better situational awareness means you're no longer reacting when something has already happened, and it's too late by then; it means that you're in-tune and present, always aware of what's happening as it unfolds.

EQ gives you control over your thought process too. The way you form your thinking directly impacts the emotions that you feel. If you were already feeling angry, for example, allowing your mind to run free with thoughts that feed into your anger is only going to make matters worse. It requires a lot of self-control, but one way of regulating your emotions is to exercise some control over your thoughts. Controlling what you allow yourself to think will make it easier for you to dissociate and remove yourself from the overpowering force of negative and unpleasant emotions. When you can remove yourself from the equation, making rational and more objective decisions becomes much easier.

The easiest way to start controlling your thoughts is by meditating. I know, you've probably heard that a thousand times, but it's true, I have experienced it myself and can assure you that it helps. Try to start meditating daily, and you'll notice how your awareness of all thoughts running through your head improves significantly.

An emotionally intelligent team is a team that embodies trust, efficacy and participation. When there's trust, greater and more effective work relationships between the leader, team members, and colleagues can exist. This paves the way for collaboration and cooperation to take place as each member believes that they work well together as a team.

Setting the Team Norms

As the leader, you get the opportunity to set the norms for your team. Start based on the following Druskat and Wolff philosophy: *"It's not always about having team members who are working through the night trying to meet deadlines. It's about THANKING them for doing it. It's not about discussing ideas in depth. It's about asking the quiet member of the group what they think. It's about acknowledging when there is unexpressed tension, false harmony, and treating everyone with respect."* Moving forward, this should be the new norm that every team member is encouraged to follow.

Encourage Relationships with Other Teams

Employees who work and play together stay together as a team. Bonding with colleagues encourages *interpersonal relationships* not just with each other but with other teams within the organisation too. Organise lunches, meetings, and friendly get-togethers with other departments regularly so everyone can get the opportunity to know each other.

Encourage Team Respect and Understanding

Encourage your team to put their phone, tablet, or papers away and *show mutual respect* for each other by prioritising face-to-face interaction. Treat everyone in the office with respect, trust, and appreciation. Be courteous, compassionate, and caring, encouraging your team to treat each other the way they would like to be treated, and promote a sense of empathy.

Supplying the Right Resources

If you want your team to learn about emotional intelligence, then you need to ensure all the resources are on hand for them to learn about it. Talk about EQ often with your employees, show them useful books, so this becomes a norm among your team.

Inter-Departmental Understanding

A core EQ skill is empathy and the ability to walk a mile in another's shoes to *understand what they have to go through* on a daily basis. Give your team the opportunity to learn about how the other groups in the organisation work and what their strategies are. That way, the next time they need to collaborate on a project, they're fully aware of what the other party needs to deal with instead of just focusing on the self-interest of their team alone.

Don't Be Afraid to Be Vulnerable

Vulnerability is not a sign of weakness, but it is an emotion that is often feared. Vulnerability is about risk. It is about uncertainty. It is defined as the possibility of being harmed or attacked, either emotionally or physically. Being vulnerable is a terrifying prospect for some. The very idea of leaving themselves open to the possibility of being hurt is enough for them to put their guard up and build emotional walls around themselves. This is an attempt to protect themselves and it is perfectly understandable. Nobody wants to be hurt. Nobody wants to be taken advantage of.

Not everyone experiences vulnerability, but when they do, they're *afraid* of letting it show. Even more so if they happen to be in a position of power, like a leader. Putting on a brave face all the time can be exhausting, both mentally and physically. Somewhere along the way, you developed the belief that if you show your weak side, people might take advantage of it or, worse, you open yourself up to being hurt. But that is *not true at all.* On the contrary, being open to the idea of letting your vulnerability show can be *liberating.* You need to show your vulnerable side because as terrifying and scary as it is, you need to know that you can count on some of the relationships you have in the moments when you need it the most. There is a quote by Brene Brown that says: *"Vulnerability is the core, the heart, the centre, of meaningful human experiences."*

A vulnerable leader is someone that people admire. It takes tremendous amounts of courage to be vulnerable, and emotional intelligence is going to give you the courage not to be afraid. People appreciate authenticity, and they respect you, even more, when you're 100% genuine with them instead of trying to be something that you're not. When you can fully admit you don't have all the answers, that you don't know

CHAPTER 6

How a Focus on Organisation Will Increase Contribution

A company that is organised will always yield a productive team. Whether it's the team leader or only an individual with the capacity to lead, someone must be ensuring the entire team stays well-ordered. It is the only way to enhance contribution while simultaneously streamlining productivity. If people know where and when to share their valuable insight, then they will feel more inclined to do so. Nowhere does a team thrive better than in an environment where they feel nurtured and supported, in an environment that has a purpose and a clear, distinct direction, one that is organised.

Organised Cultures Bring Out the Best

A team needs a purpose. The purpose is about having meaning in our lives and the things that we do. It's about staying engaged when things are tough, and it's about connection. It's easy for a team to lose connection with what they do, the people they work with, the reason they come to work, it's easy to lose sight of a lot of things if you don't have a purpose. When you don't know where the end destination is, how can you know which path to take?

Your team needs its own story. They need to find their "why." Why are they working as hard as they are? Why do they need to do the tasks that they do? Why did they come to work this morning? Why are they in this meeting? Knowing your reason why, is how you remind yourself to keep moving forward. Employees only are able to commit 100% when they can connect the things that they do to the end goal, especially during the most difficult moments. When you have a clear reason for doing what you're doing, you're never in doubt, and you always know why you must persevere.

Having a goal is one thing, reaching it is another one. That's where being organised comes to play; without a plan of what to do and when, you will never achieve your goals. Now, organisation is not to be confused with micromanagement. Micromanagers focus on the "how," rather than the "why." They tell people how things should be done instead of telling them why they should be done. Leaders focus on the result (why) but with a plan of how to work together as a team to achieve that specific goal. A successful team is extremely organised and efficient, which is how they get things done, but they do this without being micromanaged. They've been given the flexibility to arrive at the end result in a way that works best for them while staying organised at the same time.

If we look at how the world is changing around us, we will begin to notice that the organised teams and individuals are the people who accomplish more in a day than the rest do. They are the ones who seem to have it all together. The ones who smash through one task after the next until they finally accomplish all that they set out to do, and they do this while making time for themselves, their hobbies, their passions, their family, and their friendships.

An organised team is thriving at what they do, and they get things done twice as fast as teams who are a lot less coordinated because they don't waste time on unnecessary discussions. They have managed to turn themselves into a cohesive work unit that only communicates on the essential points: Efficiency, motivation, commitment, and passion. All these elements are what help to shape and mould an organised culture that brings out the best in its people, under excellent leadership too, of course.

The Secret Habits of a Highly Organised Team

Every leader wants their team to be successful, and there are many definitions of success. For some, it's about creating great products or serving customers well, for others, it's about profitable growth. No matter what your team's definition of success is, it's the leader's responsibility to set the right things in motion so the desired result can be achieved. You could have all the best strategies up your sleeve, but your ability to execute on your strategy, and thereby reaching your goal, is dependent on your team and how organised they are.

Accountability falls to you whether your team is organised or not. Having accountability means you are responsible for ensuring the success of that goal, you own that goal, and you take pride in knowing that this goal is only going to make you better, stronger, and more successful when it's done. In other words, if you care about the success of your organisation, you need to encourage your team to *be organised.*

A structured team also needs a leader who is organised in the first place. There is nothing worse than a leader who is scattered all over the place. Remember that everyone is looking to you for guidance, even if they are remote. It is you that they take their orders from. A great leader is one who is clear on what the organisation's goals are and what needs to be achieved. The leader communicates these goals with the rest of their team, so everyone is working towards the same thing. You need to rally your team around goals that have been clearly defined and take ownership of those goals. Devise a plan to turn those goals into reality together.

There are certain habits that highly organised individuals, leaders, and teams live by. They are a huge reason why these teams and individuals are successful. These habits are:

- They're proactive
- They give themselves a daily goal
- They create a system that works
- They don't let distractions get to them
- They always have a backup
- They eliminate bad habits
- They manage their expectations
- They live by their to-do lists
- Values are practiced throughout the team
- They focus on efficiency rather than excuses

They're Proactive

Success and innovation don't just happen on their own. You need to *make them happen*. Everyone knows what they're supposed to do and why their role matters, but they also need to act accordingly. People are better focused, more motivated, and they even become a lot more creative when they're not stressed out. Stress can make them feel like their work-life is a mess. When all you see is clutter surrounding your life, you can't help but sometimes feel hopeless, wondering how it came to this. These feelings will be amplified over time if nothing is done about the mental and physical disorder around them (in terms of projects and paperwork that keep piling up). As the cluster grows, so too do your feelings of misery and despair. Being proactive prevents this stress because you actually get your work done before it starts piling up.

They Give Themselves a Daily Goal

Daily goals are the easiest way to beat procrastination. When it's clear what work needs to be done at the end of the day, you know exactly what you have to do, and there's *no excuse for not working* on these tasks. Breaking your big goals into smaller chunks also makes it easier to see progress and build momentum. Instead of standing in front of a massive goal, you're now working on manageable exciting tasks and getting closer to reaching your larger goals every single day. Every member of the team needs to set a daily goal even if the task at hand may be something small, training themselves to wake up each day with a goal and the intention to get things done is what helps them get into the organised mindset and way of thinking.

They Create a System That Works

Productive people don't want to lose all that hard work they've done so far, so a team that is organised understands how important it is to always have a system that works. *Keeping your files safe and secure* is not a problem anymore with the myriad of tools available. Saving documents and backing up your data digitally is the greener way to go, in fact. Successful and organised leaders understand this, and that's why they choose to store information in a system that they trust, and they encourage their team to do the same. Apps like *OneNote*, *Google Drive*, and *Evernote* that have redundant servers across the world keep your data safely backed up. Storing information digitally also makes it much easier to share information with every member of the team quickly and easily, with the added bonus of being able to access the information anytime and anywhere you need it.

They Don't Let Distractions Get to Them

Distractions are everywhere, but organised people have mastered the art of blocking them out and not letting it bother them. If you want to *be productive*, you're going to have to do the same and remove all causes for temptation when you need to buckle down and get something done.

Start with cleaning up your working place. Get rid of all the clutter on your desk that could distract your attention from the task you're working on. The same goes for digital distractions; close unnecessary tabs and put your phone somewhere you can't see it. Also, try to create as much silence in your work environment as possible. If you're working at home, find a quiet place and let everyone know that you don't want to be disturbed while working. In an office, throw on headphones and play some white noise or calm, lyric-free music to maximise your concentration. It's essential to remove as many distractions as possible, especially if there's an important task that needs to be attended to.

They Always Have a Backup

A quick rule of thumb to remember is this: If running out of something is going to cause an interruption in your life, make it a practice to keep backups of critical items where feasible. Organised people and teams always have a backup of the essential items they need to stay productive, so if they ever run out of something, they've still got a spare on hand that is ready to use, and *no precious time gets wasted* in the process. For machines and other expensive material, a good backup plan is to rent or borrow the items from a neighbouring organization (business, school, government agency) rather than buying in duplicate.

They Eliminate Bad Habits

For positive change to happen, habits need to change first. You can't aim to have a new, organised way of working as a team if you still stick to your former bad habits. Encourage your team to get rid of old thought patterns that made them feel stressed, unproductive, and demotivated in the past and replace them with thoughts that will surge them forward on the path to success. What you're trying to do now is break the cycle, which means ditching all those bad habits that once stopped the team from reaching its full potential. Set rules to help you make decisions and commit to them. Old ways may feel comfortable, but they *may not be the most effective*. Sticking to the agreed-on norms is the best way to eliminate a lot of confusion and miscommunication. Remember, the team needs to all be on the same page if they are going to work together as a unit.

They Manage Their Expectations Wisely

Disappointments and rejection can be too much for some people to handle, especially if it seems to happen a lot. When it looks like you're facing more rejection than you can manage, it can be off-putting, and that's when confidence begins to fade away. An organised team manages their expectations to *minimise the disappointments*. They fully understand what they need to do and what the realistic outcomes might be. Setting unrealistic expectations is just another way of purposely setting up for failure. When your employees know what to expect, they're less likely to feel demotivated and want to give up.

They Live by Their To-Do Lists

Organised people are never without a to-do list. There may be a lot to do, but the key to doing it all is to pace yourself right from the start. The sluggishness as the day progresses can be the biggest challenge to overcome, and it's going to be even harder to do if you don't get things organised with a to-do list.

Encourage every member of the team to create a collective and personal to-do list of everything that needs to get done for the day. *Long-distance runners don't exhaust all their energy supply as soon as they leave the starting line.* They start at a steady pace and maintain that momentum, so it's enough to sustain themselves until they reach the finish line. Successful teams start the morning with their most demanding tasks and slowly work their way through the list progressively. Without a to-do list, before you know it, half the day is gone, and you've barely made a dent in your tasks.

Values Are Practiced Throughout the Team

This helps to foster an environment of trust within the team. Values like honesty and respect hold people accountable, and the team is able to *bond over the values* that they have set together as a team. Being aligned and practicing the same values fosters a sense of unity, and knowing that you can depend on each other to get the job done is a great feeling.

They Focus on Efficiency Rather Than Excuses

A team that is motivated and organised finds ways to increase their productivity by minimising the time spent working on activities individually when they can be grouped together. That's where the to-do list comes in handy. Viewing the list of items written down, it's easy to see which similar tasks can be grouped and work on simultaneously, so you *don't double your workload by going back and forth*. They don't make excuses for why they couldn't get something done because they hold themselves accountable. It's easy to put off unpleasant tasks, but organised people know that is just an excuse to procrastinate. If there's no concrete reason why you shouldn't start something, then don't look for excuses not to do it.

Being Organised Keeps Your Team Productive

Did you know that the average person will spend <u>one year</u> of their life looking for lost or misplaced items? Imagine the compounding effect of that in an organisation and what would happen if *every member of the team* spent a year of their life on average looking for lost or misplaced work documents. Organised people very rarely just go with the flow. Instead, they prefer to be organised and plan a list of things that they need to get done for the day, the week, or even the month. It's how they stay on track towards achieving the goals they set for themselves, and how they always seem to get more stuff done than those of you who are, say, not as productive as they should be.

"If I cannot do great things, I can do small things in a great way." ~Martin Luther King, Jr

People coming together with the same idea *can make change happen*. They can make a difference. That is what your team needs to be reminded of, and what they need to believe. Your team is a unit. They are a community in the office, and if they can learn to harness that collective power *and* build the consistent habit of staying organised and productive, there's no end to the accomplishments they could achieve. When organised, people set a goal for themselves, they're not just setting a goal; they're making a commitment to seeing it through. This commitment is what helps them to stay productive because, in the end, they don't care how long it takes or how hard they have to work, as long as they get the results that they want.

The Time-Saving Factor

When everyone knows what needs to be done, no time is wasted going back and forth with *unnecessary communication about who should be doing what*. As soon as you start the day, you and your team already should have an idea of everything that must be done that day and who should be doing it. Otherwise, you could end up spending too much time talking about delegation and trying to decide how to best distribute your tasks. By the time you reach the end of the day, not everything has been completed, and the entire team starts to get stressed. Every single moment that is not being fully utilised is another moment that is wasted. Every minute and every hour counts, and when you're organised, the time-saving factor is one of the most significant benefits that you'll gain as a team.

Minimal Stress

Even better, stress could potentially be eliminated altogether if a team works well enough and is organised. Sometimes, it can be overwhelming, trying to keep track of all the tasks on your own. That's why organised teams have a system that works for them. A system where all the information they need is stored in a shared database, ready for access at any time. Your team members are still people at the end of the day; not everyone feels productive at the same time. Some do their best work in the morning, others at later times in the day. It doesn't matter when they might be feeling that *burst of motivation*, as long as the tasks get done, and everyone has done their part. Encourage your team to make the most out of their productivity streak, find the times when they feel the most energetic and productive, and choose that time to make the most of the tasks scheduled.

Deadlines Acknowledged and Understood

Organisation breeds responsibility, seldom do you find these traits alone. A team that is organised is one that fully acknowledges and understands deadlines that must be met. There is clarity about what needs to get done, who needs to do it, and when it needs to be finalised. The communication around these deadlines is clear, and every member of the team is going to do their part to make sure these deadlines are met. Deadlines exist at the workplace for a simple reason: *Because things need to get done.* A team that is organised and productive will be able to meet these deadlines without much difficulty. Then, the company is delighted because it means operations can progress smoothly and on schedule, which leads to satisfied clients who get what they pay for.

Organisation Means Less Clutter

People often spend extra time creating clutter when they feel as though they are not organised. Greg McKeown, author of the bestselling book *Essentialism: The Disciplined Pursuit of Less* believes that people today are so focused on the concept of "more" that we take on unnecessary things we don't need. This ends up cluttering our lives and eventually making a mess that leads to lower levels of productivity.

Here's the problem with taking on too many things at once. When you underestimate the timeframe needed to complete the tasks that you take on, *you end up compromising on a lot of things*. You compromise on the quality because you're then rushing to meet the deadlines that have been set. You compromise your focus because instead of concentrating on doing your best for each task, you're now focused on racing against the clock, so that you don't miss your deadline. Instead of excelling or achieving success, you're now burned out, worn out, stressed, and still left with the feeling that you could have done better. Clutter is a distraction, and the organised mindset requires that anything which is not useful or contributing productively, needs to go.

You Make Money

Ultimately, that's the goal of every business. A company is only as successful as their employees who work for it. When you're disorganised, nothing gets done. When work is neglected, the clients are unhappy. Unhappy clients are not paying clients. When you're organised, you'll all get more done and sometimes even deliver *before* the specified deadline. Meaning you have happy and paying clients, and thus, the business ends up making more money. One of the best things about being organised and productive is that you can see the efforts your hard work has accomplished. The result of a goal that you've set out to do, and then achieved, will be hard to ignore. You'll feel proud each time you think about what you have accomplished because you did that, and you did it all by choosing to be more organised and therefore more productive.

The Leader *and* the Team Become More Influential

When you're one of the few teams in your company displaying signs of organisation and increased productivity, it's only a matter of time before other employees begin to notice. They'll wonder what you're doing right and how your team successfully achieves goal after goal. Positive morale at the workplace is essential to keep employees motivated, and other organisations will soon start looking to you for inspiration. Perhaps even ask for your guidance to point them in the right direction.

Oh, Don't Forget About Self-Discipline

A lack of self-discipline among your team can turn into a major setback. Your team may have the intention to achieve great things. They have the aim to be successful. They have the intent to meet all their deadlines and more. The problem is, they might be struggling with the self-discipline aspect of it, which only further highlights the need for organisation and purpose. If your team does not have a system, and they are flitting from day to day with no real purpose or goal in mind to work towards, they won't be achieving anything of real significance. They have no idea how to get to where they want to be. To get your mind focused on heading in the right direction, it needs a distinctive driving force that will continuously push it to keep going and not stop until the finish line has been reached.

Self-discipline is about your mindset. It is about how your brain has been programmed to work, and that is something a lot of teams struggle with today. Another problem that we all secretly struggle with is instant gratification. This is the reason why so many have fallen off the road to success. It starts with scrolling through social media and getting these dopamine rushes instead of beginning the work you should actually be doing. The thought of having access to instant gratification, instead of sacrificing and waiting for that pleasure to present itself in the future, is a thought that not many are able to resist. Resisting it isn't possible if we don't have the self-discipline needed to help us along the way.

If goals that are too big and feel overwhelming is something that your team is struggling with, help them cope by encouraging them to create a shift in their mindset; *by focusing on the change that they want to happen.* Embrace the change that they want to see, and soon, they will find themselves acting in alignment with that change. Remind them that nothing worth having is ever going to come easy or be handed to them on a silver platter. Without the challenge and stress of failure, we wouldn't have the chance to grow. I think learning to embrace this discomfort as part of the journey is how you stay motivated and disciplined enough to keep putting one foot in front of the other.

Each time your employees embrace discomfort, they're working on building and strengthening that self-discipline mental muscle. Better yet, encourage them to embrace persistence too.

Persistence can be a surprisingly rewarding emotion, because each time that you force yourself to see a task through, the result is going to make you feel much happier and better about yourself. As part of this ripple effect, that feeling is going to drive you to want to do more, to see just how far you can go if you only just persist on a task. Persistence makes victories that much more valuable. If success always came easy, we would never appreciate it as much.

CHAPTER 7:

Set Your Team Free

ou are at the final stage of becoming a great team leader. You've laid the groundwork, taken all the steps that you need to set your team up for success. Now, this last leg is just as crucial as all the other steps you've learned so far. Once you've done everything that you can as a leader, you need to *trust your team and set them free.* Yes, this means a complete release of any attempts at control and absolute trust in their abilities to get the job done. Each member of the team has been given their position because they are the best fit to conduct those actions, and this should be sufficient to allow them to do those things on their own. Do not micromanage in any way, or you will lose your team's trust and coherence. They will crumble if you insist on telling them exactly how not to do their job. Remember this; great leaders don't micromanage or control, they *lead*.

You've given the members their vision and their purpose. You've given them a goal, and you've encouraged them to embrace their differences and work together as a team. You've given them all that they need to coral around a joint mission and band together to overcome the odds as a team. You, being their leader, now need to tap into the most powerful emotional tool you can tap into. *Trust.*

The Value of Trust

If your team feels like you trust them, then they will be more willing to put their neck out for you and go the extra mile. Trust and respect go a long way in successful and effective leadership. It is the most important thing in human relations. Without trust, there is no possibility of working together well. For a leader to be considered a successful leader, that leader would always need to cultivate an environment of trust when they are with their team. A team should trust each other and know, without a doubt, that they can put their full confidence in their leader to always have their best interest at heart. This is what makes a happier, more positive team all around.

Trust your employees to get the job done, and they will. Trust them, and they will trust you in return. What does a trusting team look like? Let's look at an example. The Four Seasons Hotel in Las Vegas is a beautiful hotel. The reason is not because of the fancy beds; any hotel can buy an elegant bed and have brilliantly decorated rooms. No, the reason it is a beautiful hotel is because of the people who work there.

When you walk through the halls of the hotel, you get a distinct feeling that the people working in the hotel said hello, not because they *had to* say hello as part of their jobs. It's because they *wanted* to say hello. That's the difference, and we're more attuned to the emotions of others than we think we are. We can tell the difference between forced great customer service and genuinely excellent customer service. When the person serving you is being funny and engaging, and they love what they do, you can tell in the service that they provide. It shows in their beaming smile and helpful personality.

There's a big difference between "like" and "love." It's easy for someone to say I like my job. I like the people I meet. I like the challenge that my job brings. But *love* is emotional. If you were to ask your team right now whether they loved their work or what they thought about it, how many would tell you they *love* what they do? If they can tell you that they love what they do, then you're doing something *right*.

A leader or manager can do one of two things as they walk past their employees throughout the workday. The first is, they can ask their employees how they are doing, trusting that they're carrying out their responsibilities. Second, they can walk past their employees, checking on work without acknowledging the employee's feelings or needs. Which leadership approach works best? The answer is the first one because, with that style of leadership, you're allowing your employees to *feel* like they can do their best. The first approach is going to provide your customers with a profoundly different experience than the second one. Not because of the employee, but because of the *leaders*.

It is the leaders who are responsible for creating an environment where the employee feels like they can be themselves. A disgruntled employee will already be going through a range of emotions. And this will show in the kind of work they produce and the service they provide to the customers. Leaders often ask, *"How do I get the most out of my team?"* Your team is not a used towel; you're not trying to wring as much as you possibly can out of it before you toss it in the laundry. They are *people with feelings.* The *right question* to ask instead is:

"How do I create an environment where my team can work at their best naturally?"

The answer is trust. That is how you produce an environment where your team feels safe enough to step forward and say, *"I'm sorry, I've made a mistake."* Because mistakes happen, they are a part of how we learn on the job and get better.

You've made many mistakes when you were learning the ropes toward becoming a great leader too. Mistakes happen because we are not perfect and never will be. All you can do each day is to try your best to do your best, and that's all that you can ask from your team too. It isn't going to help anyone to be overly critical each time there's a slip or wrong move made. Your employee is probably beating themselves up enough already and anxious about the mistake they've made. They're feeling stressed and worried about it, and the last thing you should do is make them feel even worse. That's not the way to build trusting teams.

Trust your team enough to be accountable for what they are doing and responsible enough to raise their hands and say, *"I'm not sure what I'm doing; I need help."* Tell them to see mistakes as an experience to learn, and to think about what they would do differently should they be faced with such a situation again. Give them the room they need to step back, assess the situation objectively, see the mistakes they have made, and then work on how they could have handled the situation better. They need to be comfortable enough to speak up without fear of retribution. They need to trust that speaking up is not going to put them on the shortlist for the next round of layoffs if they were to reveal their vulnerable side or weakness.

Show your team that you trust them enough to handle the responsibility they have been given and that you trust them enough to be confident to speak up when they need help. They need to believe that when they ask for help, it's not a sign of weakness, that if they were to ask for help, their team and their leaders would come running to their aid. That is what a trusting team should be. That's the kind of team that is on their way to achieving success. Most employees can't tell you what they even *think* good leadership looks like, but they can immediately tell you what bad leadership *feels like*. You don't want to be the latter.

When trust among a team does not exist, then all you're left with is a group of secretly unhappy people who are coming to work each day, faking and lying their way through just to cash a paycheck at the end of the month. If trust among a team does not exist, your team is certainly not going to tell you when they've made a mistake or when they need help with what they're doing. When trust among a team does not exist, your team is going to hoard the information they have, keeping it to themselves for fear that someone else might get the glory for their ideas. Without trust, that is going to be the team culture, and over time, your team will eventually crumble. It's inevitable.

You've probably experienced yourself firsthand what lousy customer service feels like, but most of us never stop to ask *why* the employee is reacting that way. Why does the employee fake a smile? Why do we feel like we're on the receiving end of the employee's frustration? Why does the employee treat us like nothing more than just another paying customer they can't wait to serve and be done with, instead of treating each other like fellow human beings? If you stopped to ask them, the answer you would probably get in return is that *if they don't do what they're told and follow the rules, they could lose their jobs*. That tells you all that you need to know. That kind of fear among employees means they're not secure in their careers. They're not happy in their profession, and their managers or leaders don't trust them enough to do the job they have been trained and hired to do. That's what happens when trust is lacking in a team and its leader. The employee becomes more focused on protecting themselves from getting into trouble with their company instead of focusing on providing a great experience for the paying customer and doing their job well.

There's a reason why people enjoy and love flying with Herb Kelleher's Southwest Airlines, and it's not because the company has a magic formula or somehow got lucky and hired all the best people they could find. It's because the people who work there feel safe enough in their own team (you'd probably feel safe expressing yourself too if your boss came to work dressed like a rabbit). And they think that their leaders trust them enough to do their jobs. You want to have organisations that believe their leader because he doesn't micromanage them all the time. Learn to leave your employees alone once you've given them a task to work on, but make sure you're always around just in case they need help.

How to Build Trust in the Workplace

Your team needs to trust that they can come to you for the bad stuff, too, not just the good. Sometimes, the bad could include any complaints or concerns that are personal and may not be related to work at all. It might seem like no big deal to you, but to your employee, their complaints are a very big deal indeed. Challenging or dismissing their claims is only going to make matters worse, and you won't inspire much confidence in the leadership department when you do.

Work is not always going to be a smooth ride, and there will be challenges along the way to achieving a goal. Sometimes, the employee just wants someone who will listen to them. They want to know that their opinions and their feelings matter. They make an effort to come into work each day and give it their best, and in return, they just want to know that they are important to the management. As a leader, you can make them feel better by simply acknowledging their concerns and empathising with what it is they might be going through.

Being adaptable and flexible will be two of the best skills at your disposal to start encouraging and building trust among your team. Showing your team that you're willing and ready to make the necessary adjustments just to accommodate their request and make them feel better will leave a lasting impression. When an employee feels grateful and happy, their motivation and productivity levels will benefit as a result. Encourage your team to come to you whenever they have a problem and when they do, *thank them for it*. If you think about it, the employee trusted you enough to come to you with their complaints, hoping for a solution, and you should thank them for that trust to let them know you appreciate it. Not only will they be taken by surprise, but you would have successfully appeased an otherwise frustrated employee with those two simple words alone.

Be supportive of them in any way that they need. There may be times when listening alone is all the support they need. At other times, empathising and offering a solution is the support your employee is looking for. Actively listening is important here, since it gives you an idea about the kind of support they might need. If a sincere apology is in order, don't hesitate to give it. A simple *"I'm sorry for your situation"* or *"I'm sorry you had to deal with that, let me see what I can do to help,"* can do wonders to appease your employee's emotions. It lets your employee know that you are sincerely sorry about the discomfort or inconvenience they may have experienced, and this sincere attempt at understanding them will not go unnoticed.

Trust starts with the awareness of yourself. You should be tuned in and know yourself because if you're not, you won't be aware of how other people are experiencing you. When you know yourself, you're aware of everything that is going on around you. Your sense of self-awareness is heightened, and you start tuning into the different feelings you experience, possibly even recognising emerging patterns. You begin to gain insight into what makes you work and what makes your team function well together. When you're self-aware, you become intentional about everything that you choose to do. You're now consciously aligning the choices that you make with your purpose and that of your team. When you do, your full potential as a leader is unleashed. The effects of this are going to spill over into your team, and this is why emotional intelligence is such a prized leadership skill to have.

Discourage Gossip

Trust cannot exist if one person is always worried that others in the group are talking about them behind their back. Office gossip, worrying about whether you can fully trust your co-worker is an additional and *unnecessary distraction* that many people don't like dealing with. Working with so many different personalities means there is bound to be a clash of some sort. You're not going to get along with everybody, and not everyone is going to like you.

When you work in a team, you must be able to trust each other if that dynamic is ever going to work. Set the example by discouraging office gossip and not partaking in it yourself. When you hear gossip floating around, find its source and let the whole team know you're shutting it down. Let them know they can come to you if there's something they need to get off their chest, but refraining from the gossip about each other is a norm of the team that you expect them to respect.

Be Consistent in Your Approach

To be effective, you must be consistent in the way you do things; be consistent in your treatment and your rewards, be consistent in your methods of leadership, and be consistent in your principles. For example, schedule consistent catch-up sessions that are done other than through email. If some members of the team happen to work remotely, pick up the phone or connect over a video call to make the conversation more natural. You *can* add variety to hold people's attention, but keep the format consistent, otherwise the changes are distracting and potentially confusing. If the employees notice you are inconsistent in your approach, they will lose trust in you.

Keep an Open Mind

A team with no trust is a team that conceals their weaknesses and mistakes from others. They are the team that is hesitant about giving constructive feedback because it could backfire on them. A team with no trust is a team that is doomed to fail because they'll lack the ability to tap into the skills of the people they're working with and vice versa. Why do they do all this? Because their leader is not capable of listening with an open mind.

Listen with an open mind, and you'll *be more receptive to what you're hearing*. Being biased or opinionated is a form of distraction. The minute you start getting judgmental and distracted with your own thoughts, your active listening abilities are compromised. If your team feels like you are willing to give, receive and listen to criticisms with an open mind, in the long run, it will benefit everyone (both leader and the team) because when you know what the weaknesses are, you can work to improve them. And that is what being successful is all about.

Praise Them Genuinely

Learn to care about the people on your team genuinely. The best leaders have a high consideration factor, and they care about their people. It's not enough to compliment your employees when they've achieved a job well done. If the praise is not genuine, they will see straight through it. Before you can get to the point where your team feels appreciated, you must start to *genuinely* appreciate them. If you can learn to get to that point, your employees are going to notice. Once they see how you really care about the way they feel and the way you don't want anyone to feel hurt by another's action, they'll eventually learn to follow in your footsteps.

Invest in Their Development

If you want to keep your team together, it is critical to invest in their development. People want to work in a company where they are empowered to learn, grow, and develop their skills—an environment where they can *explore their full potential*. When your team feels like you're invested in them because you trust them, they'll become more engaged and be motivated to work even harder so as not to let you down. Investing in their development shows your team that you favour promoting from within. And it shows that you will reward those who have put in the hard work. It's a sign that you recognise and appreciate all they have to offer, and you're willing to invest in that to see how much further they can go. Your team is going to appreciate the trust that you have in their abilities; investing in your people is going to be one of the smartest leadership decisions you can make.

Don't Be a Micromanaging Nightmare

One of the best things you can do as a leader is to let your people do things the way they want. As long as the final product fits the desired result, allow them to work at a pace and style that they are comfortable with. Nobody likes to be micromanaged, and if they do, then they are probably too professionally immature to be working on a productive team. What is micromanagement? How do we really define it? Micromanagement could be posited as taking great, through. Sometimes, they need more time to work on a job, and that's understandable when you juggle multiple things at a time. That's why trust between a leader and their team is so important. A good leader measures performance based on the results of the work that is produced, not on how many hours your employee spends chained to their desk in a day.

Why should you stop micromanaging your team (if that is what you're doing)? Because failure is not a bad thing, *setbacks should be thought of as a benefit.* This is the last thing you would probably expect, but here is why it works. If you think about the past challenges and difficulties that you faced, which you managed to overcome eventually, instead of looking at the downside, consider the takeaway lessons each setback left you with. Did it make you a much stronger person? Did it turn out to be a blessing in disguise? Did it add something of value to your life in a way you might not otherwise have had the opportunity of experiencing? If you give your team the chance to view each setback as a gift instead of a demotivating element, you will do wonders to transform their persistence and levels of motivation to do better. Failure and setbacks are beneficial in the long-term for the smart and imaginative people who are trying to complete the mission at hand.

Failure here becomes an achievement, a main step upon the improvement of your team. If you don't give your employees at least some freedom to find their own way to get the result, then this is highly demotivating. Even worse, it might be so frustrating for them that they lose their desire to do any work at all and their productivity levels drop. Once they do, it's hard to ignite the spark that has died out.

Micromanaging your team is sending them a message that you don't trust them, that you're not confident in their abilities to do what they were trained to do. Micromanaging your team puts them in an emotional battle between wanting to keep their job and wanting to leave because they feel that they're not being valued enough where they are. Being in a state of frequent emotional turmoil can lead to stress, which, as we all know, is never good for the team. If you're micromanaging your people, it needs to stop. It's okay that you want to control results, and you need to do that because it is your responsibility to make sure work gets done so the business can keep running. But it's *not okay* to specify and control every tiny little step towards the results. There is only one solution to micromanagement: *Trust your team enough to set them free.*

Before we head to the conclusion, please let me know what you think about this book, I would really appreciate your review! Not only will it help me, but also everyone who's considering buying it. Just click the link below (or scan the QR code), it will take you directly to the review page. Thank you, it means a lot!

Amazon.com/review/create-review?&asin=B08HTF1JLH

Conclusion

ncredible accomplishments are possible when great teams work together in harmony. There's magic in different personalities coming together and working together to create a final result that everyone can be proud of. Great teamwork is the result of cooperation and the willingness to work together, embrace, and fit into the strengths and the weaknesses of other people. It's about commitment and the choice that is made every day to keep showing up for the people who are counting on you—the decision to continue being accountable for the needs of the collective, not just your own. Great teamwork is about contribution, about recognising that you may need to sacrifice some of your self-interests for the greater good at times. There is no *"I"* in the word team, and that means every member must be willing to give up the "me first" approach to reach the full height of what "we" can accomplish.

What it takes to *become* a great team is extraordinary but entirely possible at the helm of great leadership. There's no better feeling in the world than working alongside your team and coming out triumphant. To have worked hard, strived, fought, and sacrificed. To accomplish something that could only be done because you worked together is a remarkable feeling. There's nothing quite like it. That's the beauty of teamwork and how greatness is shaped.

As incredible as Michael Jordan's accomplishments are, he could not have done it on his own without the support of his team and coach (leader). Warren Buffet may have a brilliant mind, but his accomplishments are magnified because of the contributions and abilities of the people who work with him. This is the magic of collaboration. A truly inspiring leader can create a team that is able to look beyond the individual to focus on the collective and see the unbelievable talent of the unit as a whole. We know many successful people and the stories they have written. The legacy they have left behind. One of the reasons behind it all? *Teamwork.*

Finally, I encourage you to use the information from this book and put it into practice. It's now your turn to create a better work environment which will lead to better teamwork and overall more success. Don't wait, start creating your own legacy right now!

PS: If you haven't done already, don't forget to write a quick review right here. It only takes 60 seconds and would make me incredibly happy.

The Most Critical Core Values of a Successful Team

(Never lead a team without these 7 values…)

<u>Why is it important to set Team Values?</u>

Values define what your company cares about. They represent the goals and intentions of an organisation, and tell employees how their work spirit should look like. If the wrong values are set, overall productivity and work relationships will get damaged.

To receive your Team Values List for **free**, visit this link:

https://starkingbooks.activehosted.com/f/1

Personal Notes

Sources

6 Characteristics of a Bad Leader Everyone Hates! (2015, December 16). Retrieved from https://atmanco.com/blog/leadership/6-characteristics-of-a-bad-leader/

7 Organisation Stats You Need To Know. (2018, March 20). Retrieved from https://pickupplease.org/7-organization-stats/

8 Ways to Improve Diversity in the Workplace. (2016, November 28). Retrieved from https://hrdailyadvisor.blr.com/2016/11/28/8-ways-improve-diversity-workplace/

10 most ruthless leaders of all time. (2016, May 5). Retrieved from https://economictimes.indiatimes.com/people/10-most-ruthless-leaders-of-all-time/mao-zedong/slideshow/52120229.cms

Ainomugisha, G. (2019, August 12). The Importance of Emotional Intelligence in Leadership. Retrieved from https://inside.6q.io/emotional-intelligence-in-leadership/

A quote from Tao Te Ching. (n.d.). Retrieved from https://www.goodreads.com/quotes/46410-a-leader-is-best-when-people-barely-know-he-exists

A quote from The Art of War. (n.d.). Retrieved from https://www.goodreads.com/quotes/811415-the-general-who-does-not-advance-to-seek-glory-or

Baer, D. (2016, June 14). How Only Being Able to Use Logic to Make Decisions Destroyed a Man's Life. Retrieved from https://www.thecut.com/2016/06/how-only-using-logic-destroyed-a-man.html

Benefits of Keeping Organised At Work. (n.d.). Retrieved from https://www.monster.ca/career-advice/article/benefits-of-keeping-organized-at-work

Bennett, A. (2016). *Case Study: The Great British Diversity Experiment*. Retrieved from https://www.sport.wales/files/b5392774eee97dccc5b0082a767417a2.pdf

Boyd, D. (2020, February 20). Workplace Stress. Retrieved from https://www.stress.org/workplace-stress

Chignell, B. (2019, July 31). Six reasons why fun in the office is the future of work. Retrieved from https://www.ciphr.com/advice/fun-in-the-office/

Cortez, S. (2013, March 12). Anyone Who's Unemployed Should Spend At Least 20 Minutes Doing This Task. Retrieved from https://www.businessinsider.com.au/how-being-organized-affects-productivity-2012-6?r=US&IR=T

Emergenetics International. (2018, April 11). The Connection Between Vulnerability and Trust in Teams. Retrieved from https://www.emergenetics.com/blog/the-connection-between-vulnerability-and-trust-in-teams/

Emotional Intelligence in Leadership: Learning How to Be More Aware. (n.d.). Retrieved from https://www.mindtools.com/pages/article/newLDR_45.htm

Essentialism - The Disciplined Pursuit of Less by. (2019, April 23). Retrieved from https://gregmckeown.com/book/

Evans, B. D. (2020, February 6). Most CEOs Read A Book A Week. This Is How You Can Too (According To This Renowned Brain Coach). Retrieved from https://www.inc.com/brian-d-evans/most-ceos-read-a-book-a-week-this-is-how-you-can-too-according-to-this-renowned-.html

Freiberg, K. A. J. (2019, April 7). 20 Reasons Why Herb Kelleher Was One Of The Most Beloved Leaders Of Our Time. Retrieved from https://www.forbes.com/sites/kevinandjackiefreiberg/2019/01/04/20-reasons-why-herb-kelleher-was-one-of-the-most-beloved-leaders-of-our-time/#57ce5869b311

Gallup 2019 Global Emotions Report - Gallup. (2020, April 8). Retrieved from https://www.gallup.com/analytics/248906/gallup-global-emotions-report-2019.aspx

Hafezi, S. (2019, December 6). Are You Having Fun at Work? Retrieved from https://www.achievers.com/blog/are-you-having-fun-at-work/

Heath, V. (2019, July 29). Debate: Does diversity training work? Retrieved from https://www.gendereconomy.org/does-diversity-training-work/

Holmes, M. (2019, September 5). Why are there so few women CEOs? Retrieved from https://theconversation.com/why-are-there-so-few-women-ceos-103212

How to build trust at work. (n.d.). Retrieved from https://www.monster.com/career-advice/article/6-steps-to-building-trust-in-the-workplace-hot-jobs

G. (2019, June 3). Understanding the Differences: Leadership vs. Management. Retrieved from https://www.go2hr.ca/retention-engagement/understanding-the-differences-leadership-vs-management

Gleeson, B. (2016, November 9). 10 Unique Perspectives On What Makes A Great Leader. Retrieved from https://www.forbes.com/sites/brentgleeson/2016/11/09/10-unique-perspectives-on-what-makes-a-great-leader/#41ca1c165dd1

FORTUNE EDITORS. (2014, March 20). The World's 50 Greatest Leaders. Retrieved from https://fortune.com/2014/03/20/worlds-50-greatest-leaders/

Insight: What Dictators Have in Common. (n.d.). Retrieved from https://www.vision.org/insight-what-dictators-have-in-common-8859

Jenkins, R. (2020, February 6). The Underestimated Productivity Factor of Diversity and Inclusion. Retrieved from https://www.inc.com/ryan-jenkins/the-underestimated-productivity-factor-of-diversity-inclusion.html

Johnson, I. (2018, February 7). Who Killed More: Hitler, Stalin, or Mao? | Ian Johnson. Retrieved from https://www.nybooks.com/daily/2018/02/05/who-killed-more-hitler-stalin-or-mao/

Kottasova, I. (2014, December 1). Foreign name? Expect a tougher job hunt. Retrieved from https://money.cnn.com/2014/12/01/pf/jobs/foreign-names-jobs-discrimination/

Landry, L. (2019, April 3). Emotional Intelligence in Leadership: Why It's Important. Retrieved from https://online.hbs.edu/blog/post/emotional-intelligence-in-leadership

Leadership Lessons from Cicero. (n.d.). Retrieved from https://www.luther.edu/ideas-creations-blog/?story_id=515847

Levy, C. P. (n.d.). Self-Discipline, a Must for Team Success | General Leadership. Retrieved from https://generalleadership.com/self-discipline/

M. (2020a, April 16). Improving Emotional Intelligence (EQ). Retrieved from https://www.helpguide.org/articles/mental-health/emotional-intelligence-eq.htm

MacKay, J. (2018, March 1). How to set smarter daily goals –. Retrieved September 4, 2020, from https://blog.rescuetime.com/daily-goals/#:%7E:text=Daily%20goals%20bring%20a%20level,I%20feel%20more%20in%20control

Metz, T. (2019, April 22). 5 Key Takeaways from Jeff Bezos' Leadership Style. Retrieved August 11, 2020, from https://pagely.com/blog/5-lessons-from-jeff-bezos-leadership-style/

Miller, C. C. (2018, April 24). The Top Jobs Where Women Are Outnumbered by Men Named John. Retrieved from https://www.nytimes.com/interactive/2018/04/24/upshot/women-and-men-named-john.html

Myatt, M. (2012, October 22). 15 Ways To Identify Bad Leaders. Retrieved from https://www.forbes.com/sites/mikemyatt/2012/10/18/15-ways-to-identify-bad-leaders/#25a908c715da

One third of your life is spent at work. (n.d.). Retrieved from https://www.gettysburg.edu/news/stories?id=79db7b34-630c-4f49-ad32-4ab9ea48e72b&pageTitle=1%2F3+of+your+life+is+spent+at+work

Orchestrating Impartiality: The Impact of "Blind" Auditions on Female Musicians | Gender Action Portal. (2020, March 1). Retrieved from https://gap.hks.harvard.edu/orchestrating-impartiality-impact-%E2%80%9Cblind%E2%80%9D-auditions-female-musicians

Peshawaria, R. (2012, July 28). There Is No Such Thing As Bad Leadership. Retrieved from https://www.forbes.com/sites/rajeevpeshawaria/2011/08/19/there-is-no-such-thing-as-bad-leadership/#6afa76d07b43

Play is an innate emotion in the brain, important to understanding autism, adhd, and child development. (n.d.). Retrieved from http://mybrainnotes.com/autism-adhd-play.html

Powers, A. (2018, June 27). A Study Finds That Diverse Companies Produce 19% More Revenue. Retrieved from https://www.forbes.com/sites/annapowers/2018/06/27/a-study-finds-that-diverse-companies-produce-19-more-revenue/#49100807506f

Profile in Leadership: Amazon Founder Jeff Bezos. (n.d.). Retrieved August 11, 2020, from https://www.jacksonvilleu.com/blog/business/profile-in-leadership-amazon-founder-jeff-bezos/

Rampton, B. J. (2018, February 13). 7 Ways to Create Emotionally Intelligent Teams. Retrieved from https://execed.economist.com/blog/guest-post/7-ways-create-emotionally-intelligent-teams

Recruitment, C. (n.d.). 9 Ways to Promote Workplace Diversity in 2019 - Change Recruitment. Retrieved from https://www.changerecruitmentgroup.com/knowledge-centre/9-ways-to-promote-workplace-diversity-in-2019

Reynolds, K. (2019, July 10). 5 Strategies for Promoting Diversity in the Workplace. Retrieved from https://www.hult.edu/blog/promoting-diversity-in-workplace/

Strauss, K. (2018, June 21). More Evidence That Company Diversity Leads To Better Profits. Retrieved from https://www.forbes.com/sites/karstenstrauss/2018/01/25/more-evidence-that-company-diversity-leads-to-better-profits/#4a1ff8231bc7

Point/Counterpoint: Are Outstanding Leaders Born or Made? (2017, April 1). Retrieved from https://www.ncbi.nlm.nih.gov/pmc/articles/PMC5423074/

Ramos, T. (2018, November 27). Effective Leadership: Why It's Important And How It's Achieved. Retrieved from https://blog.runrun.it/en/effective-leadership/

Ryan, L. (2016, March 28). Management Vs. Leadership: Five Ways They Are Different. Retrieved from https://www.forbes.com/sites/lizryan/2016/03/27/manage

ment-vs-leadership-five-ways-they-are-different/#313a8bd269ee

T. (2018, May 2). 9 ways emotional intelligence improves team productivity. Retrieved from https://medium.com/smells-like-team-spirit/group-eq-makes-your-team-more-productive-at-work-we-have-proof-315eaa695190

Takala, T., & Auvinen, T. (2016, April 2). The Power of Leadership Storytelling: Case of Adolf Hitler. Retrieved from https://www.researchgate.net/publication/299599048_The_Power_of_Leadership_Storytelling_Case_of_Adolf_Hitler

Team, C. (2019, October 23). How to Build Emotionally Intelligent, Productive Teams. Retrieved from https://cmoe.com/blog/build-emotionally-intelligent-productive-teams/

Team, T. (2020, March 18). The Importance of Discipline in Teamwork. Retrieved from https://www.tbae.co.za/blog/the-importance-of-discipline-in-teamwork/

Team, T. O. T. (2017, December 13). How to Have Fun at Work and Why it is Important. Retrieved from https://www.the1thing.com/blog/family-health-happiness/how-to-have-fun-at-work-and-why-it-is-important/

Teamwork Blog | Product Updates, Customer Stories & Company News. (n.d.). Retrieved from https://www.teamwork.com/blog/

Thiran, R. (2013, March 29). It Pays To Have Fun At Work! Retrieved from https://leaderonomics.com/leadership/it-pays-to-have-fun-at-work

Thomas, A. (2020, February 6). 15 Traits of the Worst Leaders (Avoid at All Costs). Retrieved from https://www.inc.com/andrew-thomas/15-traits-of-the-worst-leaders-avoid-at-all-costs.html

The Difference Between Leadership and Management. (n.d.). Retrieved from https://www.nextgeneration.ie/blog/2018/03/the-difference-between-leadership-and-management

Tracy, B. (2019, August 13). 6 Time Management Skills For A Productive Life. Retrieved from https://www.briantracy.com/blog/time-management/6-

time-management-tips-to-increase-productivity-organizational-skills/

Sexton, C. (2017, June 19). 7 Reasons Why Being Organized Boosts Productivity. Retrieved from https://theproductivityexperts.com/7-reasons-why-being-organized-boosts-productivity/

Strategic Leadership: The Essential Skills. (2019, March 12). Retrieved from https://hbr.org/2013/01/strategic-leadership-the-esssential-skills
STRESS FACTS. (2018, December 12). Retrieved from http://www.gostress.com/stress-facts/

Stress symptoms: Effects on your body and behavior. (2019, April 4). Retrieved from https://www.mayoclinic.org/healthy-lifestyle/stress-management/in-depth/stress-symptoms/art-20050987?reDate=18052020

The Leadership Lessons I Learnt From Niccolo Machiavelli. (2017, December 8). Retrieved from https://leaderonomics.com/leadership/leadership-lessons-machiavelli

Three Differences Between Managers and Leaders. (2014, August 7). Retrieved from https://hbr.org/2013/08/tests-of-a-leadership-transiti

Thomas, A. (2020, February 6). 15 Traits of the Worst Leaders (Avoid at All Costs). Retrieved from https://www.inc.com/andrew-thomas/15-traits-of-the-worst-leaders-avoid-at-all-costs.html

What Are the Characteristics of a Good Leader? | CCL. (2020, April 27). Retrieved from https://www.ccl.org/blog/characteristics-good-leader/

What Is Emotional Intelligence, Daniel Goleman. (2020, April 15). Retrieved from https://www.ihhp.com/meaning-of-emotional-intelligence

Why diversity matters. (n.d.). Retrieved from https://www.mckinsey.com/business-functions/organization/our-insights/why-diversity-matters

Why Diversity Programs Fail. (2019, October 15). Retrieved from https://hbr.org/2016/07/why-diversity-programs-fail

Why Having Fun at Work is Important. (n.d.). Retrieved from https://www.kellyservices.us/us/careers/career-resource-center/managing-your-career/why-having-fun-at-work-is-important/

Workforce Diversity: A Key to Improve Productivity. (2014, January 1). Retrieved from https://www.sciencedirect.com/science/article/pii/S2212567114001786

Y. (2020, February 18). 15 Traits of a Terrible Leader. Retrieved from https://www.success.com/15-traits-of-a-terrible-leader/

Zitelmann, R. (2019, November 4). The Jack Ma Story: Why Thinking Big Is More Important Than Technical Knowledge. Retrieved August 11, 2020, from https://www.forbes.com/sites/rainerzitelmann/2019/11/04/the-jack-ma-story-why-thinking-big-is-more-important-than-technical-knowledge/#7ee32b70419c

Zojceska, A. (2020, April 3). How to Build, Manage and Promote Workplace Diversity? Retrieved from https://www.talentlyft.com/en/blog/article/246/how-to-build-manage-and-promote-workplace-diversity

Printed in Great Britain
by Amazon